Discerning The Spirits

of This End Time Apostolic Age

John Arcovio

Foreword By Billy Cole

Discerning the Spirits of this End Time Apostolic Age
by John Arcovio

©1998 Spirit Led Ministries Publishing

All scripture quotations are from the New King James Version of the Bible unless otherwise noted. Bold and italic types are for authors' emphasis only.

All Hebrew and Greek translations of biblical terms are taken from *Strong's Hebrew and Greek Lexicon*.

Cover artwork by Mann Chuan

Published by Spirit Led Ministries Publications
3214 North 35th Street, St. Joseph, MO 64506
1-816-279-5866 voice
1-816-279-3357 fax

Visit our Web Site at http://www.spiritled.org

All rights reserved under International Copyright Law. No portion of this publication may be reproduced, stored in an electronic system, or transmitted, in any form or by any means, electronic, mechanical, photocopying, recording, or otherwise without the prior written permission of the author.

ISBN 978-0-9647343-3-3

Printed in the United States of America

First edition July 1998
Second March 2007

See back page of book for information on ordering ministry resource material's by John Arcovio

Dedication

Discerning the Spirits of this End Time Apostolic Age
is dedicated to the thousands of spiritual pioneers, warriors, and giant-killers who have passed to this generation the legacy, truths, and spiritual principles we hold so dear.
When someone looks at a mighty rushing river with awe and admiration, he must remember that the river, with all of its magnificent beauty and power, is simply following a course that was carved out centuries before. Some of the greatest outpourings of the Spirit of God in the history of mankind are occurring in this generation.
We give honor to our elders and pioneers who blazed the trails before us.
May each soul that receives the Holy Ghost both domestically and internationally honor your efforts and sacrifice. Thank you for preserving and passing on this inheritance to us. We will guard these truths and spiritual principles with our very lives!

TABLE OF CONTENTS

Foreword
Acknowledgments
Scripture Text
Preface

1. The Spirit of God 4

2. Angelic Spirits 34

3. Demonic Spirits 71

4. The Human Spirit...93

5. Epilogue: The Spirit of This Age 106

FOREWORD
ACKNOWLEDGMENTS

I am very pleased with the young men God has anointed in this hour in prayer, intercession, seeking the will of God and practicing the gifts of the spirit. Brother Arcovio is such a person. He is very sincere in seeking the will of God for his life and to be used of the Lord. He has paid the price in prayer and fasting.

Brother Arcovio is an important part of the special team that travels with me to my crusades each year. He is very skillful in practicing the gifts of the spirit and in the operation of the Holy Ghost. He is not a novice. He is not only powerful and mightily used in the gifts of the spirit, but he is balanced with genuine love, compassion, kindness and mercy...a good balance. He is being used of God successfully across the world in crusades where thousands are receiving the Holy Ghost.

The truths and spiritual principles written in this book will be a blessing and strength to all who read it.

W.H. (Billy) Cole
Charleston, West Virginia

A special thank you to Brother Billy Cole for the investment of time, training, and mentoring you has put into my life and ministry for the past seven years. I pray that every domestic and international crusade the Lord allows us to conduct will bring honor to you, sir.

Andrea, Jonathon, Ariella, and I love and appreciate you. Thank you for your love and support throughout the years.

As always, the greatest thanks is to Jesus. You make all things possible in our lives.

SCRIPTURE TEXT

*While we do not look at the things which are seen, but at the things which are **not seen**. For the things which are seen are temporary, but the things which are not seen are eternal.*
-2 Corinthians 4:18

Preface

As the coming of the Lord approaches and we prepare to cross the threshold into the 21st century, it is my conviction that the Church must possess the operation of the gift of discerning of spirits. Paul mentioned this gift in his first letter to the Corinthians, writing, "To another the working of miracles, to another prophecy, to another *discerning of spirits*, to another different kinds of tongues, to another the interpretation of tongues" (1 Corinthians 12:10).

If we ever prayed for any of the gifts of the spirit to operate in our lives, we need to pray for the operation of the gift of discerning of spirits. Every pastor must pray for it as he leads the sheep. Every evangelist must pray for it as he schedules meetings and ministers in the end-time harvest. Every prophet must pray for it as he imparts, directs, equips, and ministers to the body of Christ. Every teacher must pray for it as he trains and grounds both the new believers and the mature saints in the ways of God. Every apostle must pray for it as he pioneers new works and leads the Church into deeper waters of apostolic revival. And each and every believer must pray for it as the curtain begins to fall upon this present age.

Concerning this matter of spiritual discernment, the apostle John wrote, "Beloved, do not believe every spirit, but test the spirits, whether they are of God; because many false prophets have gone out into the world" (1 John 4:1). It is imperative that we "test" the spirits of this age through the operation of discerning of spirits to avoid the deceptions and ambushes of the enemy.

Paul also wrote in his letter to the church in Corinth, "Lest Satan should take advantage of us; for we are not ignorant of his devices" (2 Corinthians 2:11). We must develop a greater understanding of the unseen dimension of the spirit realm which God has made available to us for warring against the spiritual principalities, powers, rulers, and hosts of wickedness of this age. For this to happen, we must become sensitive to the voice of God.

Ever since I was a child, God has enabled me to be very sensitive to the spiritual realm. I can remember God speaking to me at the young age of ten or eleven as I walked through the woods where we lived in the hill country of Oak Hill, Texas. He spoke in a voice that was so clear it almost seemed audible. In this final hour when countless deceptive voices are all around us, every man and woman of God must learn to discern and obey the true voice of God.

The Lord impressed me to write this book after a dream I had while in England in June of 1996. In this dream, I found myself in a large warehouse with high, dirty windows. Through these windows I could see a devastating war in progress. In the center of this cobweb-covered warehouse was a group of women and children huddled together. Around the perimeter of the building stood a contingent of men who were doing their best to protect their families from the attack of the enemy.

Through the hazy windows I could see the enemy, dressed in army fatigues and armed to the teeth. As I looked around to assess the defensive strength of the men protecting their families, I saw, to my dismay, that all they had to fight with were little pocket knives and small cap pistols.

As I jumped down to join the battle I screamed, "Don't you have any long-range weapons? The enemy is closing in on us!" At that moment, I saw the shadowy form of one of the enemy soldiers swinging on a rope. He suddenly came crashing through one of the windows causing great confusion and alarm. It was only then that I looked down at my feet and noticed weapons of all sorts lying on the ground around us. I hastily picked up a hand grenade and, being inexperienced with this kind of weapon, pulled the pin. I immediately threw it toward the enemy soldier, not realizing I was supposed to wait a few seconds before I threw it. The soldier nonchalantly picked up the grenade and tossed it back toward me. I awoke from my dream to the blast of the grenade lifting me off my feet and into the air.

As I awoke I found myself trembling and weeping, my body covered with sweat. I fell out of bed and onto my face, crying out in anguish unto the Lord. After a few minutes, the Lord spoke to me in that still, small voice saying, "You must instruct my people that not only must they obtain the 'long range' weapons of my Spirit through prayer and fasting, they must also learn how to use them properly. They must not wait until the enemy comes crashing into their living rooms, corrupting their children and destroying their marriages, before they discover my weapons in the unseen dimension of the Spirit."

Brothers and Sisters, we must obtain the weapons of warfare that make us mighty through God now! We can wait no longer!

The spirits we will examine in this book are as follows: the Spirit of God, angelic spirits, demonic spirits, the spirit of man, and the spirit of this age. I pray that the scriptural truths compiled in this book, along with the many supernatural encounters I have experienced throughout the past fifteen years, will impact you with a greater understanding of the benefits God has made available to you in the unseen dimension of the spirit realm.

John Arcovio

The Spirit of God

Samuel, Samuel," the voice called out, echoing through the quiet temple and awaking the young man out of his sleep. Springing to his feet and rushing into the quarters where Eli slept, Samuel answered, "Here I am, for you called me." Stirring groggily from his deep sleep, Eli whispered, "Go back to bed Samuel, I did not call for you." With a confused look, Samuel slowly returned to his cot in the corner of the instrument room and lay back down.

> **"Samuel, no matter what others do, you keep your heart clean before God and do all you can to serve and obey both the Lord and the man of God".**

Just as he was drifting back to sleep he again heard the voice echoing off the white walls and pillars of the temple, "Samuel, Samuel." It was unmistakable. Once again Samuel leapt from his cot ready to serve the man of God. Rushing breathlessly into Eli's quarters he repeated his previous statement, "Here I am, for you called me." With an annoyed look, Eli rose up on one elbow and opened a sleepy eye. "No Samuel, I did not call for you. Now go and lie down like I

Spirit of God

told you to before." Slowly Samuel returned to his cot to lie back down.

Things had not been going well for Samuel lately as life at the temple serving the priest was not all it was cut out to be. Samuel wished that Eli would teach him more about the things of God and how to know the voice of God, for he did not yet know the Lord, neither was His word yet revealed to him. As a matter of fact, there was no open revelation anywhere in the land. As a child he could remember the daily devotions to Jehovah and teachings his mother gave him. Now it seemed that he was only taught how to do the simple daily chores around the temple.

The tasks he performed that should have held meaning, such as filling the brazen laver with water or emptying the ashes from the brazen altar, held no meaning at all. It even seemed as though Eli performed the sacred rituals with apathy. To make things worse, Samuel often witnessed the wicked deeds of Hophni and Phinehas, Eli's sons. He so missed his mother, Hannah. During her occasional visits he tried to tell her about the things he saw Eli's sons doing and how God could not possibly be pleased with them. But the only reply he received was, "Samuel, no matter what others do, you keep your heart clean before God and do all you can to serve and obey both the Lord and the man of God." She would then recount the story of how she had dedicated him to the Lord even before he was conceived, vowing that she would give him up to serve the Lord all the days of his life. The story always comforted Samuel, especially when he felt the loneliest and most confused.

Samuel lay on his cot trying futilely to return to sleep. But with such profound questions racing through his mind, he could not. Were Hophni and Phinehas playing yet another of their tricks on him? Where was this voice, which he was sure he was hearing, coming from? He tossed and turned like a ship on a restless sea. Finally he forced himself to lie completely still and listen to the crickets performing a symphony of nature's music outside the window. Their performance was suddenly interrupted by the recurring voice, "Samuel, Samuel." There was no mistake this time. He had heard the voice clearly and distinctly while laying wide awake.

Cautiously the boy walked into Eli's quarters and tentatively said, "Here I am, for you did call me." Eli started to reprimand him for waking him the third time when, somewhere in the cobwebs of his distant memory, stirred the recollection of a time when he heard the voice of the Lord in a similar way. It had been so long since the Lord had spoken to him that he had all but forgotten how to recognize the voice of God. Rising slowly from his bed, the old man called Samuel to his side. Apologetically he said, "Samuel, all I have ever taught you was to know my voice and commands. My son, it is the Lord God Jehovah who is speaking to you." Eli then instructed Samuel saying, "Go, lie down, and it shall be, if He calls you, that you must say, 'Speak, Lord, for Your servant hears.'" Samuel turned, his heart beating heavily, and mused, "The LORD GOD JEHOVAH is speaking to me?"

Spirit of God

Laying back down on his cot, he nervously awaited for the Lord to call for him again. Soon the Lord came and, standing before him, called as he had before, "Samuel!

> **"Samuel, all I have ever taught you was to know my voice and commands. My son, it is the Lord God Jehovah who is speaking to you."**

> **"Relationship is the foundation for divine communication."**

Samuel!" Looking up, Samuel suddenly saw a translucent glow coming from the far corner of his room. Sitting up trembling, the lad answered, "Speak, for Your servant hears." Then the Lord said to Samuel, "Behold, I will do something in Israel at which both ears of everyone who hears it will tingle. In that day I will perform against Eli all that I have spoken concerning his house, from beginning to end. For I have told him that I will judge his house forever for the iniquity which he knows, because his sons made themselves vile, and he did not restrain them. And therefore I have sworn to the house of Eli that the iniquity of Eli's house shall not be atoned for by sacrifice or offering forever."

As abruptly as it had arrived, the visitation of the Lord departed. Visibly shaken by this prophetic message of wrath from God, Samuel paced back and forth across the floor for over an hour. Finally he eased back into bed.

Samuel lay sleepless for the rest of the night. As the purple and lavender fingers of the dawning sun stretched slowly across the valley, Samuel arose and opened the doors of the house of the Lord. He usually enjoyed sitting in the temple courtyard, drinking a cup of hot goat's milk while watching the birds flit playfully in the brazen laver. He enjoyed listening to the different sounds of life preparing for another day. On this morning, however, he was so perplexed by the divine message that he could only numbly start his daily chores.

Being afraid to tell Eli of the vision, for most of the morning Samuel avoided any contact with him. Around noon Eli called Samuel saying, "Samuel, my son!" Samuel timidly answered, "Here I am." Eli paused thoughtfully before saying, "What is the word that the Lord has spoken to you? Please do not hide it from me. God do so to you, and more also, if you hide anything from me of all the things that He said to you." Samuel reluctantly walked into the room and sat down before his superior. Taking a deep breath, he proceeded to tell Eli everything, holding back nothing. After a long silence, Eli said, "It is the Lord. Let Him do what seems good to Him."

* * *

Notice that the Word of the Lord was not revealed to Samuel until he had developed a relationship with God. Relationship is the foundation for divine communication. It is evident from the Scriptures that the intimacy of this relationship and communication with God only deepened as time went by:

So Samuel grew, and the Lord was with him and let none of his words fall to the ground. And all Israel from Dan to Beersheba knew that Samuel had been established as a prophet of the Lord. Then the Lord appeared again in Shiloh. For the Lord revealed Himself to Samuel in Shiloh by the word of the Lord (1 Samuel 3:19-21).

The Lord revealed himself to Samuel through the communicated Word during the times of their "walking together." In like manner, we can become sensitive to the voice of the Lord as we invest quality time alone with Him, seeking His face.

It is imperative that we first be able to discern the Spirit and voice of God before we attempt to distinguish the other spirits and voices that are present around us. People who handle money are taught to become intimately familiar with real currency so that the moment their fingers touch a counterfeit bill they will know it. This same principle applies to the discerning of spirits: Once we become familiar with the Spirit of God we will then be in a position to accurately discern the other spirits and voices.

In my world travels over the past ten years and being in contact with various men of God, ninety-nine percent of them have told me that the primary way God speaks to them is through the "still small voice." This is also how God speaks to me. I have come across a few whom God speaks to through a loud, audible voice or some other unique means, but this is the exception and certainly not the rule.

We then can seek to "learn" the still, small voice and its subtle impressions as the means by which the Lord will speak to us. There is much trial and error involved in learning to recognize the voice of God. Understanding this, we should always allow the written Word to confirm and govern

> **The Lord spoke the devil and his host into existence and could just as easily speak the devil and his host out of existence!**

anything we feel God is speaking to us.

An initial truth we must understand is that *all spirits* are created by God. Colossians 1:16 tells us: "For by Him all things were created that are in heaven and that are on earth, visible and invisible, whether thrones or dominions or principalities or powers. All things were created through Him and for Him."

This is especially important to remember when dealing with spiritual warfare. The Lord spoke the devil and his host into existence and could just as easily speak the devil and his host out of existence! All things were created "for Him!" This means that no matter what the enemy accomplishes, it is all still in accordance with the permission and ultimate plan of God.

Clearly it was the devil working through evil men who arrested and crucified Jesus. Yet the Bible tells us that He was "delivered by the determined purpose and foreknowledge of God" (Acts 2:23). The crucifixion was the eternal plan of God, yet He brought it to pass through the hands of corrupt men and malicious spirits. In the Old Testament we find an account where God even uses a lying spirit to further His ultimate plan:

> *Then Micaiah said, "Therefore hear the word of the Lord: I saw the Lord sitting on His throne, and all the host of heaven standing on His right hand and His left. And the Lord said, 'Who will persuade Ahab king of Israel to go up, that he may fall at Ramoth Gilead?' So one spoke in this manner, and another spoke in that manner. Then a spirit came forward and stood before the Lord, and said, 'I will persuade him.' The Lord said to him, 'In what way?' So he said, 'I will go out and be a lying spirit in the mouth of all his prophets.' And the Lord said, 'You shall persuade him and also prevail; go out and do so.' Therefore look! The Lord has put a lying spirit in the mouth of these prophets of yours, and the Lord has declared disaster against you"* (2 Chronicles 18:18-22).

The vision of Micaiah may be troublesome to some since it seems to suggest that God may sometimes act as the author of deceit. This is clearly, however, just one of many examples of the sovereignty of God, who does not initiate attacks of evil spirits but sometimes allows them to occur for His own purposes. We can also observe this principle operating in the life of Job (Job 1 & 2), the life of King Saul (1 Samuel 16:14-16), and in the life of the apostle Paul (2 Corinthians 12:7-9). Yes, even the spirit activity in the enemy's realm is governed by God!

When we become intimately acquainted with the Spirit of God, all other spirits will come under subjection to the

> **When we become intimately acquainted with the Spirit of God, all other spirits will come under subjection to the authority gained through this relationship.**

authority gained through this relationship. True authority over the enemy is a result of a person submitting himself to God and His Word. As James says, "Therefore submit to God. Resist the devil and he will flee from you" (James 4:7).

Submission to God and obedience to His Word will afford authority to every believer over the wicked spirits of this age. It is every believers responsibility to mature in his walk with God that he may take authority over spirits that are harassing him and oppressing the lives of others.

All spirits must answer to, and be in subjection to, the Spirit of God, either now by choice or one day in the future

Spirit of God

by force. This truth confirmed in Romans 14:11: "For it is written, As I live, saith the Lord, every knee shall bow to me, and every tongue shall confess to God."[i] It is further supported by Philippians 2:9-11:

> *Therefore God also has highly exalted Him and given Him the name which is above every name, that at the name of Jesus every knee should bow, of those in heaven, and of those on earth, and of those under the earth, and that every tongue should confess that Jesus Christ is Lord, to the glory of God the Father.*

What a joy it is to be able to make Jesus the Lord of our hearts right now by choice rather than later when we have no choice! What a blessing to submit our spirits to His Holy Spirit! Let us gladly bow the knees of our hearts to our precious Lord and Savior!

It is vital that we understand early in our walk with God that there is only one "spirit realm." There is not one spirit realm that demonic spirits operate in and a separate spirit realm that God's Spirit and angelic spirits operate in. The Spirit of God and all other spirits operate in the same supernatural domain. This is why Paul wrote these words to the church in Corinth:

> *And no wonder! For Satan himself transforms himself into an angel of light. Therefore it is no great thing if his ministers also transform themselves into ministers of righteousness, whose end will be according to their works* (2 Corinthians 11:14-15).

The enemy uses this ability to transform himself to

deceive many who seek God through extended fasts. He is cunning when it comes to his disguises. The enemy formerly dwelled in the fiery stones of the holiness of God. Ezekiel writes: "You were the anointed cherub who covers; I established you; You were on the holy mountain of God; You walked back and forth in the midst of fiery stones" (Ezekiel 28:14). We need to know that Satan was thoroughly schooled in the ways of righteousness, though now he has plunged into the depths of wickedness. He is nevertheless very adept at making good appear evil and evil appear good. This is why we must pray for God to thoroughly equip us in the gift of discerning of spirits. This an important tool in accurately

> **This means that if you have a dream from God, you will probably eventually have a dream influenced by the enemy.**

discerning the voice of the Lord.

I recall in 1986 during a 35-day extended fast (under observation and supervision my pastor, Brother Kilgore.) that around the 28th day I was alone in the prayer room lying on my face in travail. Suddenly I became aware of a "presence" that had entered the room. I looked up and out of the corner of my eye I saw a figure standing near me bathed in radiant brilliance. I started to look directly at the figure but suddenly felt checked by a warning of the Holy Spirit. Then I distinctly felt the fear of God wash over me as a voice said, "Get up off the floor and walk directly out of this room." This voice did not have to speak twice as I literally ran from the room. To this day I believe that the enemy (appearing as an angel of light) was seeking to distract me from my God-chosen fast or even destroy me. I am so thankful I was trained by my mentors early in my ministry to always be sensitive to and obey the prompting of the Holy Spirit! (Perhaps you are wondering why I fasted 35 days and not 40. It is because I did not want to fast a full 40 days and run the risk of feeling as though I had arrived. I was concerned that as a young man I might allow pride to enter my heart, thinking, I can do what Jesus did. There are some things in the spiritual realm that are sacred and fearful to me and I will not approach unto them. Please let me caution you not to fast beyond 21 days unless God instructs you to and you remain completely under your *pastor's and doctor's supervision*.)

We must pray to be able to acutely "test" every spirit we come in contact with as John admonished:

Beloved, do not believe every spirit, but test the spirits, whether they are of God; because many false prophets have gone out into the world. By this you know the Spirit of God: Every spirit that confesses that Jesus Christ has come in the flesh is of God (1 John 4:1-2).

We test the spirits through a combination of prayer, fasting, the operation of the gift of discerning of spirits, and knowledge of the written Word of God. When we fast and pray, crossing that line of sensitivity into the spirit realm, we become both sensitive to both the Spirit of God and demonic spirits. All spirits, all principalities, all powers operate in the same dimension: what Paul called the "heavenly places." He spoke of this in his writings to the church of Ephesus:

Discerning the Spirits of this End Time Apostolic Age

To the intent that now the manifold wisdom of God might be made known by the church to the principalities and powers in the heavenly places (Ephesians 3:10).

This means that if you have a dream from God, you will probably eventually have a dream influenced by the enemy. If you see an angel, prepare yourself, for you will probably see a demonic manifestation as well. To have true authority and success operating in the spirit realm, we must obtain and manifest the wisdom of God in these potentially destructive situations. This wisdom cannot be obtained by merely reading this book (or any other book for that matter). This wisdom comes only from God. As James urged the believers of his day, so I urge you now to begin praying right away for God to give you this wisdom from above. We will talk more in chapters two and three about angelic and demonic spirits.

Those who choose to "pay the price" in fasting and prayer and succeed in entering into this supernatural realm learn (for the most part) to ignore the demonic and focus in on the things of God. If they do not, the enemy will successfully torment them with continual distractions and manifestations. Though the enemy hates to be ignored, ignoring him is often the best defense against him. In Acts 16 when the slave girl possessed with a spirit of divination followed Paul saying, "These men are the servants of the Most High God, who proclaim to us the way of salvation," Paul ignored this demonic harassment for many days before finally turning in anger and casting the demon out.

It is up to each believer to "exercise" his senses to a keen edge of operation in the discerning of spirits. Paul explained this in his letter to the Hebrews,

Spirit of God

> *But strong meat belongeth to them that are of full age* [mature, perfect]*, even those who by reason of use have their senses exercised to discern both good and evil*[ii] (Hebrews 5:14).

The phrase "by reason of use" in this verse is translated from the Greek word *hexis* (hex'-is), which means "a habit whether of body or mind, a power acquired by custom, practice, use."[iii]

Not all habits are detrimental. We can develop habits of intimacy with God through prayer and sensitivity to the voice of God through fasting, along with the disciplined development of the fruit of the Spirit, which will produce positive results in our lives. It has been demonstrated that its takes approximately 40 days for the human mind and body to form a new habit. If we choose to fast consistently one day a week for a forty-week period of time, after that forty weeks we will have formed a positive habit of fasting in our life. In like manner, if we will pray a specific amount of time every

Disciplines of the spirit can become habits if we will remain consistent in them.

day for forty days, at the end of this period we will find ourselves daily being influenced toward these newly formed habits. Disciplines of the spirit can become habits if we will remain consistent in them.

The way we become intimately acquainted with God is to spend much time alone with Him in prayer, fasting, and daily communion. The more time we spend with our maker in the "secret place," the more intimately we will know His Spirit and voice. In his book *The Power of Prayer,* E. M. Bounds wrote the following statement, "God's acquaintance is not made hurriedly. He does not bestow His gifts on the causal or hasty comer and goer. To be much alone with God is the secret of knowing Him and being of influence with Him."[iv]

This "influence' is not purchased through "bartering" our time and energy, but rather as the natural sum in the equation of intimacy and reciprocal relationship with God.

It is recorded in Psalms 91:1, "He who dwells in the secret place of the Most High shall abide under the shadow of the Almighty." This secret place, or "hiding place," can initially be found only by much time alone with God where there are no distractions. It is that sweet place in the Spirit, where the hours melt by and you are giving pure time to the One you love the most. Once you discover that "secret place" with your Lord, you will long for it time and again and will learn how to "slip" into it in any setting, driving down the highway, riding on a airplane, sitting at a desk. Once discovered, we can visit our secret place whenever we choose.

I can remember the exact time and place where I first discovered my "secret place". It was in the summer of 1985. I had just completed an extended fast of 14 days. At that time in my life, I was working on a construction crew and the work days were long (10 hours) and hot (105 degrees Fahrenheit) in the humid Texas summer. I had gone to bed early that evening at 9:00 p.m. so I would be rested for the next workday. Around 10:00 p.m. I was awakened out of a deep sleep by what felt like a light touch on my chest. As I lay there in the darkness, the still small voice of God spoke to me and said, "Why don't you go to the church and pray?"

Spirit of God

This is how God usually speaks to me, in a still small voice that could be easily missed. Some people are waiting for God to thunder from heaven with a booming voice punctuated by flashes of lightning. They often miss the true voice of God because they are not sensitive to His still small voice.

Another thing to remember is that when God speaks, He will say the same thing when He speaks again, be it the next day, the next month, or the next year. God works in the realm of eternity. He is in no rush. It is the enemy that knows his time is limited and pressures us for an immediate response. He will often "corner" a child of God and pressure him or her to make an immediate and rash decision or step of direction. The book of Revelation tells us: "Woe to the inhabitants of the earth and the sea! For the devil has come down to you, having great wrath, because he knows that he has a short time" (Revelation 22:12).

The peace of God often accompanies His voice, but with the enemy you often feel pushed or pressured. Beware of this call for a hasty decision when seeking to determine the will of God concerning important personal decisions. It is incredible what just a night spent in prayer or a few days spent fasting can do toward discerning the mind of God concerning a situation. The Holy Spirit will never harass His children over a direction or impression. All impressions from above will grow stronger as we wait on God and pray. Once you are certain you have heard from God, then boldly step out by faith and never doubt in the darkness of a night what you heard from God in the brightness of the noonday.

I recall a saint who was making a financial decision concerning a matter in which I had already told him that I felt the peace of God and encouraged him to step forward by faith. A few days later he called to reverse his decision saying, "My wife has been having tormenting dreams concerning this for seven nights straight." My reply to him was, "This must be an attempt from the enemy to distract and discourage you. The God I serve does not torment His children with dreams." He chose to ignore my advise and subsequently suffered great financial loss.

The two hardest spirits to discern as separate and distinct voices are the voice of the human spirit and the voice of the Holy Spirit. It is a very thin line that separates them. With time you will be able to very easily distinguish the voices of angels, demons, and the spirits of this age, but it will take awhile to distinguish between your own human spirit and the voice of God. We will discuss this in more detail in Chapter 4.

When operating in the gifts of the word of wisdom, the word of knowledge, and prophecy, I often wait until the word is spoken to me at least three times before I step out to speak it. This is one safeguard against mistaking a word from the human spirit as a word from God. If a word is impressed on me while I am preaching and after several minutes is not repeated, I continue preaching and it usually passes. This, to me, means it was only a word generated out of my own human spirit or discerned emanating from another human spirit. This happens often when ministering to someone who is consumed with a desire for a certain thing (for example, a barren woman desiring a child). What happens is her human spirit will "scream" in desperation with this desire. This is also true when a word is impressed on me and I forget it within a few minutes. A true word from God does not become lodged in your mind but placed in your spirit. The Holy Spirit does not forget!

Spirit of God

People often mistake the voice of their conscience as being the voice of God. Our conscience "speaks" to us throughout the entire day and is strengthened by fasting, prayer, meditation on the Word of God, and obedience to God. It is weakened by continually giving in to temptation without repentance, the lack of prayer and fasting, and disobedience to the Word. On the contrary, God does not just "chatter" all day long. Whenever the Lord speaks, it is because He has something significant to say. Sometimes His words are very few, while other days He may talk to us at

> **Whenever the Lord speaks, it is because He has something significant to say.**

length, perhaps dealing with areas of our lives that He is trying to transform.

I have found that when God speaks to me concerning others, often through a word of wisdom, a word of knowledge, or prophecy, it is in short sentences or even in just a word or two. When I step out in faith and speak those few words, then very often more will be revealed to me. Often God will not give me too much more because I might be tempted to try to interpret the word incorrectly. For example, there was a service when the Lord revealed one word concerning an elder sitting on the platform. The word was "camel." When this word was spoken, then a further word was revealed, "God wants you to get off your camel." Now at that moment this word did not mean one thing to the man of God, but when it was repeated the third time with

Discerning the Spirits of this End Time Apostolic Age

more emphasis, the elder fell to the floor, sobbing in repentance. What the pastor, church, and evangelist did not know was that the elder had a secret habit of smoking Camel cigarettes and God wanted him "off his camel." The elder did get off his camel indeed and was able to successfully stop smoking without anyone ever really finding out the true interpretation of that word.

When God speaks to me concerning myself or my family, He usually speaks longer and in more detail. The most memorable times of conversation occur after the third or fourth hour of prayer and waiting in His presence. Long after the "voices" of daily plans and schedules have faded away, His still small voice quietly emerges. This is why I love all-night prayer meetings alone in a church building. At 3:00 or 4:00 in the morning there are no interruptions. Because most people are in bed asleep, the spirit realm has quieted down tremendously. Often, after an hour or so of simply lying on my back on the carpet and just singing in tongues, He will come and oh, what a blessed communion! We often converse for hours while time seems to stand still. On these occasions I can bear my heart before Him and He can deal with the most delicate issues of my heart of hearts. Often in those precious moments, I wish the whole world, with its pressures, responsibilities, and schedules, would just vanish away and I could stay there in intimate fellowship forever. Oh, how I long for that day when the trumpet will sound and I can sit at His feet! I know that I will wash His feet with tears of love and thankfulness. I will be selfish and refuse to leave His side.

Spirit of God

In my life there have been a few men of God whom I have been moved to wash their feet simply because they reflected the nature of the Jesus we serve. One songwriter expressed it this way, "Oh I want to see Him, look upon His face...." The more time we spend in His presence, the more we can understand the heart cry of Paul in Philippians 3:10, "That I

The only problem with having a "pity party" is that nobody else shows up.

---

may know Him and the power of His resurrection, and the fellowship of His sufferings, being conformed to His death." It will only be when we reach the place where we truly "know the Lord" that we will become intimately acquainted with His voice.

The prophet Elijah discovered that the Lord often speaks in the "still small voice." In First Kings, Chapter 19, Elijah had gone out into the wilderness to flee the wrath of Queen Jezebel. He was at a very low point in his life, no doubt suffering from a low self-image. His trust and faith in God had "bottomed out." He had what I call a "cave mentality," feeling that he was all alone, the only one suffering, the only one walking this path of loneliness. The only problem with having a "pity party" is that nobody else shows up. Fortunately for Elijah, the Lord decided to show up at his pity party. Lets look at the scriptural account of the meeting:

> *And there he went into a cave, and spent the night in that place; and behold, the word of the Lord came to him, and*

Discerning the Spirits of this End Time Apostolic Age

He said to him, "What are you doing here, Elijah?" So he said, "I have been very zealous for the Lord God of hosts; for the children of Israel have forsaken Your covenant, torn down Your altars, and killed Your prophets with the sword. I alone am left; and they seek to take my life."

Then He said, "Go out, and stand on the mountain before the Lord." And behold, the Lord passed by, and a great and strong wind tore into the mountains and broke the rocks in pieces before the Lord, but the Lord was not in the wind; and after the wind an earthquake, but the Lord was not in the earthquake; and after the earthquake a fire, but the Lord was not in the fire; and after the fire a still small voice. So it was, when Elijah heard it, that he wrapped his face in his mantle and went out and stood in the entrance of the cave. Suddenly a voice came to him, and said, "What are you doing here, Elijah?"(1 Kings 19:9-14)

The word "still" in verse 12 is translated from the Hebrew word d^emamah (dem-aw-maw'), which means silence, whisper, calm.^{v} Elijah did not discover the Word of the Lord in the wind (what he could hear with his human ears) or in the earthquake (what he could feel in his human emotions) or in the fire (what he could see with his human eyes). He found the Word of the Lord in the still small voice. In like manner, when we seek to discover the still, small voice of God, it will not be discerned by our natural hearing, our eyesight, or our human emotions. It will be discovered within our human spirit as we quiet ourselves and become "still" before him. Obviously we cannot listen and talk simultaneously. It must be one or the other.

To discern His voice requires disciplined time just sitting

Spirit of God

before Him in complete silence, simply waiting on Him. If we will spend 15-20 minutes each week in the quietness of His presence, not speaking or praising, just sitting and waiting upon Him, His voice will be revealed to us. The more we spend time in His presence and the more we get to know him, the more we will realize how little we really know about Him. We then learn to simply quiet ourselves in His presence that we might know His voice and learn of Him. We must know Him.

I have learned that whenever I'm in the presence of holy men of God such as Brother T. W. Barnes, Brother James Kilgore, Brother Billy Cole, or Brother Kenneth Haney, I sit quietly and listen to what they have to say. How much more when I'm in the presence of the King of Glory!

Some people never learn to recognize the voice of God because when they are in His presence *they dominate* the entire conversation. David wrote one of his songs of ascents:

Lord, my heart is not haughty, nor my eyes lofty. Neither do I concern myself with great matters, nor with things too profound for me. Surely I have calmed and quieted my soul, like a weaned child with his mother; like a weaned child is my soul within me (Psalms 131:1-2).

One of the reasons David was said to be a man after God's own heart was because he would listen to the still, small voice of God. There is a vast difference between hearing and listening or hearkening. My own sweet bride can "discern" whether I am simply hearing her or truly listening to her. Spiritual understanding comes when we "listen" to His voice. The Bible says of Jesus said in Mark 7:14, "And when he had called all the people unto him, he said unto them,

Discerning the Spirits of this End Time Apostolic Age

Hearken unto me every one of you, and understand."

Once we have learned to recognize His voice, it won't matter if we are in the middle of a shopping mall or an airport terminal, He will be able to speak to us and we will be able to pick out His voice among the many voices. This reminds me of a story of a banker and an Indian scout who were friends. They were walking along in Time Square in downtown New York during the rush hour. The sidewalk was completely packed with people. Suddenly the Indian scout stopped and cocked his ear towards the side of a staircase and said, "I hear a cricket." The banker looked at him astonished and replied, "You hear what?" The Indian scout repeated himself and said, "I hear a cricket!" The banker looked around nervously as the press of people began to try to push past them. Just then the Indian scout walked over to a flower pot sitting by the staircase and scraped some leaves aside. Sure enough there was a cricket chirping merrily away in the flower pot. The banker was amazed and asked the scout, "How in this world could you hear that cricket in the middle of all of this hustle and bustle?" The Indian calmly replied, "It is all in what you are listening for." He then said, "Watch this." And taking a handful of change out of his pocket, he threw it on the ground. Every person for a city block stopped walking and turned their heads to look and see where the money had fallen.

What the Lord was trying to impress upon Elijah was that, even though He could use Elijah to call down fire from heaven or to shake the foundations of kingdoms, when all the flash and grandeur of these supernatural operations were past, it was the intimacy of walking with His Creator and knowing His still, small voice that would keep him through the lonely nights of discouragement and oppression from the enemy. We must know Him!

Spirit of God

As New Testament believers, we can learn from this account not to always be looking for a mighty manifestation of God's power to confirm His presence in our daily lives. We should be seeking to be sensitive to His presence in that still, small voice, even when we can't seem to "feel," "see," or "hear" His workings. We can also learn not to allow any emotion or circumstance to cause us to waver from doing what God has spoken to us to do. *The Bible Knowledge Commentary* makes the following comment on 2 Kings 19:11-14:

Standing on the mountainside outside his cave, Elijah witnessed what Moses had seen in those mountains centuries before (Ex. 19:16-18) and what he himself had seen on Mount Carmel only a few days earlier (1 Kings 18:38, 45), namely, a spectacular demonstration of the power of God, this time in wind, an earthquake, and fire. But on this occasion the Lord was not in any of these, that is, they were not His instruments of self-revelation.

Evidently some time later when Elijah was back in his cave (19:13) he heard the *sound of a gentle whisper*. Recognizing this as a revelation of God he pulled his cloak over part of his face, walked out to the mouth of the cave, and stood there waiting for God to act. God asked the same question He asked earlier: What are you doing here, Elijah? The prophet's response was identical to his first reply, suggesting that even though he may have understood the point of God's display of natural forces for his benefit he still felt the same way about himself.

The message God seems to have intended for Elijah is that whereas He had revealed Himself in spectacular demonstrations of His power in the past at Kerith, Zarephath, and Carmel, He would now use Elijah in gentler, less dramatic ways. These ways God proceeded to explain to His servant (verses 15-18). God would deal with Elijah's personal feelings about himself later in a gentle way too.[vi]

I believe this also expresses the manner in which God would speak through modern day prophets today. Whereas the Old Testament prophets experienced a lot of natural phenomenon (i.e. fire, wind, visible hands writing on walls) in connection with the receiving of the Word of God, New Testament prophets seem to receive a word from God mainly through impressions and the still, small voice. This also makes the New Testament prophets more vulnerable to "missing" the voice of God or "misinterpreting " a true word from God (possibly one reason why we don't stone a prophet who "misses" in this day).

* * *

As I lay there in the darkness, my mind offered its silent plea, "Don't you have to get up early in the morning?" Again the Lord spoke to me and quietly implored, "Why don't you go to the church and pray." Again my mind tried to deflect the voice of God by reasoning, "Why do you have to go all the way out to the church? Why don't you just kneel right here by the side of your bed and pray for a while." Finally, the decision was made and the voice of God won the battle. I silently arose and, slipping on my pants and shirt, responded to the prompting of the Lord to meet him at the "secret place." (I believe it is important for a child of God to not only have a special "inner" secret place, but also an actual, physical secret place where he feels comfortable praying. This could be a spot in the church or a room in the house.)

Spirit of God

I recall that as I was driving down the back roads to the church, I began to feel a burden from God slowly descend upon me. Soon I was weeping so intensely under this burden that I could barley see to drive. This burden grew more intense as I neared the church. When I stepped out of the car

> **All awareness of time or external thoughts were swept away in each increasingly intensified wave of travail.**

at the church parking lot, I fell to my knees under the load of the burden. I began to crawl on my hands and knees across the asphalt pavement groaning and weeping in travail.

I crawled into the church and collapsed in front of my pastor's office door. I closed my eyes as the intense fury of wave after wave of deep travail began to sweep over me like unrelenting ocean waves. It was as though I was being pulled down a long tunnel of prayer. Lying there on the floor, twisted up like a pretzel, prolonged wave after prolonged wave of travail swept through my entire body and soul until my whole being, body, soul and spirit, became united as one in response to the intercession of the Spirit.

Travail became united with each breath I took. When one sustained wail of travail ended and I pulled in a great breath of air the next sustained travail would flow out. All awareness of time or external thoughts were swept away in each increasingly intensified wave of travail. Eleven p.m. came and went. Midnight came and went. One a.m. came and went. Hours slipped by like the waters of a swiftly moving river.

The carpet around my head became soaked with my tears and perspiration from the agony and intensity of my travail. Two a.m. slipped past. Then three and four joined the history of travailing prayer. By now a supernatural force had taken over my entire being, giving me the strength to remain focused in mind, body, and spirit.

> **I must visit this place often lest my soul become lax and the vision become dim.**

Five a.m. Six a.m. Surely I could not keep up the deep waves of travail, one after another, for much longer. Breath by breath, travail after travail, the quarters of the secret place I would visit for many years to come were being built.

At 6:30 a.m. the soft glow of dawn began to slowly inch its fingers of gold and lavender across the hallway carpet and the waves of travail began to slowly subside. When the spirit of deep intercessory travail finally lifted from me, I was completely spent. I didn't even have the strength to lift my hand off the carpet. I lay there still gently weeping as I basked in the afterglow of the Shekinah. After 30 minutes I gathered my strength to get up and go to the restroom to wash my face and try to get ready for another day of work. When I looked up from the sink, I didn't even recognize the person looking back at me. My eyes were swollen almost completely shut from weeping. My face was flushed and swollen. My lips were swollen almost twice their normal size, but I had discovered that secret place of the Most High, that place where my thoughts become His thoughts, where He shares His heartbeat and His burden with His own.

Spirit of God

This is where I first discovered what intimacy with God truly means. This is where a burden was born and a vision was ignited. I must visit this place often lest my soul become lax and the vision become dim. It was shortly after this time that I fasted a certain length of time (which I will not disclose due to the physical and spiritual dangers of this type and length of fast) that God also revealed to me the ministry of angelic spirits. We will discuss this further in the next chapter.

Psalms 91 closes with the revelation of intimacy with God, the keen awareness of His voice, and the angelic ministry one discovers when he enters that secret place.

> *For He shall give His angels charge over you, to keep you in all your ways. In their hands they shall bear you up, lest you dash your foot against a stone. You shall tread upon the lion and the cobra, the young lion and the serpent you shall trample underfoot. "Because he has set his love upon Me, therefore I will deliver him; I will set him on high, because he has known My name. He shall call upon Me, and I will answer him; I will be with him in trouble; I will deliver him and honor him. With long life I will satisfy him, and show him My salvation"* (Psalms 91:11-16).

If we are going to know His voice and His Spirit intimately, then we must hunger for that secret place. It is at the place of sitting at the feet of Jesus where true revelation of His Word and will comes. Some become so "busy" serving the Lord that they have no time to visit that secret place and sit at His feet. Their efforts become futile and their lives depleted of the power and revelation of God. It is at His feet that we are equipped to battle the spirits of this age. Jesus said in Luke 10:38-42, "Martha, Martha, you are worried and troubled about many things. But one thing is needed, and Mary has chosen that good part, which will not be taken away from her."

That which we receive in that secret place at the feet of Jesus is sealed for eternity. Nothing will ever take it from us. Oh, how we must long for that secret place!

Endnotes for Chapter 1:

i. *The King James Version*, (Cambridge: Cambridge, 1769).

ii. Ibid.

iii. *Enhanced Strong's Lexicon*, (Oak Harbor, WA: Logos Research Systems, Inc., 1995).

iv. E.M. Bounds, *The Power of Prayer*, (   ), pp.

v. *Enhanced Strong's Lexicon*, (Oak Harbor, WA: Logos Research Systems, Inc., 1995).

vi. Walvoord, John F., and Zuck, Roy B., *The Bible Knowledge Commentary*, (Wheaton, Illinois: Scripture Press Publications, Inc., 1983, 1985).

2

Angelic Spirits

The evangelist had been ministering door to door in a low-income section of town for several hours. Although the people he was ministering to and praying for spoke only Spanish, they could feel his genuine love for their troubled souls. The only words the evangelist could speak that they understood were, "Inglesia, Domingo."

This ghetto area was home to one of the fiercest gangs in all of Los Angeles. And to make things worse, the man of God was unknowingly wearing the colors of a rival gang. Stepping out of an alley onto the main street where his car was parked, the evangelist was suddenly surrounded by 20 young men. They all wore caps and jackets adorned with the emblems of the professional football team, the Oakland

Angelic Spirits

Raiders. None of the men were smiling. For a millisecond fear washed over the evangelist. Then like a flash flood, Holy Spirit boldness filled his heart. He looked at the gang leader and spoke to him with divine authority, saying, "What you men are searching for is the love of God that can only come through the infilling of the Holy Ghost."

For a moment anger flashed in the eyes of the gang leader. But then, as he glanced past the shoulder of the man of God, his entire countenance changed. He spoke something in Spanish to the gang members and they quickly parted, making a way for the evangelist to leave. The Holy Spirit then prompted the man of God to leave immediately without looking back.

When the evangelist returned to the church where he was ministering, he shared the experience with the pastor. When he got to the part about the gang members surrounding him, the pastor's eyes grew wide as he asked, "Did these men have Oakland Raiders football paraphernalia on?" The evangelist nodded yes. The pastor then further exclaimed, "How did you get out of there alive? These men are members of one of the most vicious gangs in our area. Why just last year my son was outside of our church building simply bouncing a basketball and several of the gang members walked up and slashed the side of his face open with a razor...just for the thrill of it." The evangelist could only say, "God protected me."

Two days later the same evangelist was involved in some door to door ministry about two blocks from the church when he saw the same gang leader with one other person walking down the street toward him. The evangelist approached them and greeted them, asking if they remembered who he was. They nodded in agreement. Then the evangelist asked, "Why did you choose to leave me alone even though I was in your

neighborhood wearing an opposing gang's colors?" The leader replied, " Yeah, we were going to 'do you.' But when you started talking about that spirit stuff, I got to feeling something I had never felt before. Then those two big men

> **But when you started talking about that spirit stuff, I got to feeling something I had never felt before.**

that were with you stepped out of the alley behind you. We have never seen men this huge and muscular and we didn't want to mess with them. So we let you go."

Even though the evangelist never saw them himself, the warrior angels of the Lord that stand for the children of God had intervened!

* * *

The man of God had been fleeing the wrath of government and community leaders for several weeks. His only crime was that he had publically preached the name of Jesus. He had been dragged from his pulpit by soldiers while he was preaching and beaten with a board with rusty nails sticking out of it until his scalp hung from his head by a thread of skin. The soldiers then threw him severely wounded and bleeding into a filthy jail cell with the full intent of killing him the next morning. The man of God prayed in tongues for several hours until he fell into a restless sleep. Just before sunrise a tall angel of the Lord opened the jail door and prodded him awake saying, "You are to run away until the danger is past."

The man of God got up and immediately began to run across the countryside toward the village he had grown up in, which was over 200 miles away. Weary from lack of sleep and many days without a proper meal, he entered the outskirts of a remote village in the southern region of Ethiopia. Under cover of darkness, he silently threaded his way past a group of huts until he found the one owned by a faithful sister in the Lord. He was hastily pulled into the hut and met with the silence of knowing stares.

The Apostolic Church of Ethiopia had been under severe persecution for several years. Many had lost property, houses, or church buildings to the fires fueled by the demon-inspired hatred of the communist government for these "Jesus Name people." Many had even been shot or burned alive for openly preaching the name of Jesus. Silently the man of God ate a morsel of food and drank some water. He then lay down for a few unsettled hours of sleep.

After about four hours of fitful rest, he woke with a start. The only thought that consumed his mind was, "I must continue fleeing!" Swinging his legs over the cot, he began to stand when suddenly his feet and hands felt bound together by an apparently invisible rope. He began to call out, "In Jesus Name! In Jesus Name!" as he struggled to move. What he did not know was there was an angel of the Lord standing there invisibly keeping him bound, for the angel knew what the man did not: that the soldiers who were after him had caught up with him and surrounded the village.

For seven days and seven nights the preacher sat on the cot, immaterially bound, taking no food or water, only continually calling on the name of Jesus and praying in the Spirit. Finally the soldiers left and he was loosed from his

> **The ministry of angelic spirits is not a fairy tale but a divine reality in the lives of those children of God who will dare to believe.**

unseen bonds. This incident took place more than 20 years ago, but this man of God still lives today to preach the message of the revelation of Jesus' name!

How many times have we felt 'goose bumps' when one of these true stories is recited to us? The ministry of angelic spirits is not a fairy tale but a divine reality in the lives of those children of God who will dare to believe. While the average Christian may never personally witness a visible manifestation of an angel, we can learn to discern their presence through the gift of the discerning of spirits. We should pray that God would "open our spiritual eyes of faith" to become more attuned to the spirit realm which is daily in our midst.

In Second Kings 6:15-17, Elisha prayed for God to open the eyes of his servant to see the manifestation of warrior angels surrounding the city. When the eyes of the servant of the man of God were opened, he saw that they that were with them in the spirit realm were far more than they that were against them in the natural.

Elisha prayed and said, "Lord, I pray, open his eyes that he may see." Then the Lord opened the eyes of the young

Angelic Spirits

man, and he saw. And behold, the mountain was full of horses and chariots of fire all around Elisha.

Lord, open our eyes of faith that we may "see" your host in our everyday lives. Any time we board an airplane, take a trip in a car or on a boat, enter into spiritual warfare through prayer, fasting, or ministering the Word, we must recognize and utilize the ministry of the angelic hosts. Whenever I get on an airplane, I silently pray, "God let your angels protect this flight." When I enter cities to minister there in the Word and Spirit I pray, "God, loose the hosts of warrior angels to do warfare against the principalities and powers of this city, and loose ministering and harvesting angels to draw people who need You to this meeting." We will speak in more detail about the warrior, ministering, and harvesting angels.

This reminds me of a humorous event that took place while on a flight from Hong Kong to San Francisco. Shortly after taking off we flew into a very violent storm. The winds were extremely turbulent with frequent wind shears. The wind howling outside of the aircraft sounded like a banshee. At times it seemed as though the wind was going to literally rip the wings off of the airplane. The plane's engines would scream at times from the free-spinning rpms on free falls of 50 to 100 feet at time. At other times it felt as though we were in a large boat being heaved to and fro by a storm tossed sea. Needless to say, it was a frightening situation.

I had just closed a very exhausting ten-day crusade in the country of Singapore and was wanting to sleep on the flight home. I took several pillows and curled up against the window and proceeded to drift into sleep. I did not notice the white-knuckled Asian businessman sitting next to me curiously watching me. I must have slept for several hours when I awoke, needing to use the restroom. The plane was still in extremely turbulent winds which had seemed to decrease somewhat in velocity. I politely excused myself and went to the restroom. When I returned to my seat and began preparing to resume my sleep, I noticed the businessman intently staring at me. I smiled and greeted him. He responded by saying in broken English, "You no afraid?" I replied, "No, not really." The businessman then said, "How come you no afraid?" I replied, "Oh sir, my Father owns this airline." His eyebrows rose as he said, "Ah, I see, your father very important man!" I nodded in agreement and replied, "Oh yes, as a matter of fact, every flight I take He sees to it that a special team of airplane mechanics makes certain that the equipment is in top running condition!" He looked at me thoughtfully for a few seconds and then his face relaxed as he smiled and said, "Yes, it is very good then that I am flying with you!" Laying back in his seat, he proceeded to close his eyes to rest.

I later had the opportunity to introduce my fellow traveler to my Father through the revelation of His Word. Thank you

> **Oh yes, as a matter of fact, every flight I take He sees to it that a special team of airplane mechanics makes certain that the equipment is in top running condition.**

Jesus for your fleet of "angel mechanics." Through eyes of faith I know they are there helping me every step of the way!

There have only been a few occasions when I *may have* experienced a physical manifestation of an angel. In each instance it was not until *after* the experience that I realized it could have been an angelic ministry. Paul warned us, "Do not forget to entertain strangers, for by so doing some have unwittingly entertained angels" (Hebrews 13:2).

I believe that in instances of physical angelic ministries, the Lord "blinds" our eyes and "blocks" our understanding of the experience until after it is over. This principle is also found in the story of the men walking to Emmaus:

> *Now behold, two of them were traveling that same day to a village called Emmaus, which was seven miles from Jerusalem. And they talked together of all these things which had happened. So it was, while they conversed and reasoned, that Jesus Himself drew near and went with them. But **their eyes were restrained**, so that they did not know Him* (Luke 24:13-31).

Later in verses 28-31, after a full day's journey with the Lord, it is recorded:

> *Then they drew near to the village where they were going, and He indicated that He would have gone farther. But they constrained Him, saying, "Abide with us, for it is toward evening, and the day is far spent." And He went in to stay with them. Now it came to pass, as He sat at the table with them, that He took bread, blessed and broke it, and gave it to them. Then **their eyes were opened** and they knew Him; and He vanished from their sight.*

Discerning the Spirits of this End Time Apostolic Age

The disciples spent several hours with Jesus without recognizing who He was. Then, as soon as they did recognize Him, He instantly disappeared from their sight.

In early December of 1990 I was traveling by car from Denver to Los Angeles with only two days to make the trip. As I was driving westbound on a desolate stretch of Interstate Highway between Green River, Utah, and Reno, Nevada, I realized that I was about 200 miles from the nearest building. There was nothing in front of me, behind me, or on either side

> **I slowed down and spotted the man still lying on the side of the road. The man did no move and I feared he might be dead.**

of me but dry, barren, empty desert. I had my Bible opened on the seat beside me, and I was listening to a preaching tape of Jeff Arnold. His message was on the story of the Good Samaritan. I was immersed in the message when I suddenly saw out of the corner of my eye a man lying on the side of the road on the eastbound side of the freeway. At first I was surprised at what I was seeing. I hadn't passed a single car on the interstate for over an hour. I slowed down as I pondered what to do. I was already behind schedule on my trip, but I knew that I couldn't drive on by while listening to the story of the Good Samaritan. So I turned around to see if the man needed help.

I had to drive ahead for ten miles before to found a crossover to the eastbound side of the interstate. By the time I reached the crossover my mind was reasoning that someone else had certainly stopped to help by now. Nevertheless, I made a u-turn and headed back. By the time I had reached the location where I had seen the man, nearly twenty minutes had passed. I slowed down and spotted the man still lying on the side of the road. He wasn't moving and I feared he might be dead. I rolled the passenger window down and asked, "Sir, are you ok?" He suddenly sat up, smiled, and said, "I am now, thank you."

I will never forget the dull green Eskimo style parka he was wearing. The tan fur outlined his dark-skinned face. He stood up and leaned on the half opened window and smiled again. A gust of wind swirled around him blowing a fridged blast of air into the warm interior of my car. The outside temperature was in the mid-teens. I thought to myself, "He must be freezing, lying on the cold ground in this desolate wilderness." I asked him, "Do you need a ride?" He just smiled and replied, "No, it is enough that you stopped". I asked, "Would you like to come in the car for a while and warm up?" The stranger slowly shook his head and, smiling, said, "No, it is enough that you stopped." I then asked if he needed any money and received the same reply.

I sat there dumfounded for a few seconds. Then I remembered that I had a basket in the backseat with some fruit and pop-tarts in it. I took the basket and held it out to the man saying, "Here, are you hungry?" He took the basket saying nothing, only smiling. I then said," Well sir, I have to get going. I'm on my way to Los Angeles and I'm already late."

At that moment he stopped smiling and looked straight into my eyes. He said, "And when you get to Los Angeles, you will have the breakthrough you have been praying for." I remember the steel blue eyes and how they cut right into my heart. I felt my knees go weak, and I silently wondered how he knew that I was going to preach a revival in Los Angeles. I then reasoned that he must have seen my Bible lying open on the seat. I thanked him and rolled the window up.

The man turned and, rather than walking down the freeway, turned south and walked straight into the empty desert. I started to pull back onto the freeway when the realization hit me: *That could have been an angel.* I stopped the car and turned to look at the man again. But I couldn't see him anywhere. I put the car in reverse and backed up the 25 feet I had driven forward. I then opened my door and stood on the door step looking over the top of the car, scanning the horizon of the open desert. I could clearly see for at least 1,000 yards, but no one was in sight. I left the driver's door open and the car running while I walked around the car to the ditch on the side of the road. There, five feet from the road, sat my basket with the fruit and pop tarts in it. At that moment Hebrews 13:2 came to mind: *Do not forget to*

> **The Scriptures describe angelic ministry as a vital part of every Spirit-filled believer's life.**

entertain strangers, for by so doing some have unwittingly entertained angels.

For eight years in a row now I have returned to two

Angelic Spirits

churches in the Los Angeles area and each revival has grown in magnitude and power. I believe that soon I will participate in a city-wide crusade where this message from heaven will be fulfilled!

The Scriptures describe angelic ministry as a vital part of every Spirit-filled believer's life. Angels operate for ministry, protection, and warfare on behalf of the children of God. Psalms 34:7 says, "The angel of the Lord encamps all around those who fear Him, and delivers them" (I believe the term "the angel of the Lord" always refers to the host of warrior angels). Psalms 91:11-12 records, "For He shall give His angels charge over you, to keep you in all your ways. In their hands they shall bear you up, lest you dash your foot against a stone." This verse describes the ministering angels that are sent forth to minister in behalf of those who are inheriting eternal life. As Hebrews 1:14 tells us, "Are they not all ministering spirits sent forth to minister for those who will inherit salvation?"

All angelic spirits, both those that have fallen and those that remain in the service of God, have their beginning in the creation of God. Colossians 3:16 records, "For by Him all things were created that are in heaven and that are on earth, visible and invisible, whether thrones or dominions or principalities or powers. All things were created through Him and for Him." Certainly "all things" includes the angelic host.

In the beginning there were three angelic hosts each led by an archangel. These archangels were: Michael, who was set over warfare matters of the kingdom of God; Gabriel, who was set over the messenger, ministering, and harvesting angels; and Lucifer, son of the morning, who was set over the glory and music of the kingdom of God.

The word "archangel" appears only twice in the

Scriptures, once in Jude 9 in describing Michael and once in 1Thessalonians 4:16 in describing Gabriel.

> *Yet Michael the archangel, when contending with the devil he disputed about the body of Moses, durst not bring against him a railing accusation, but said, The Lord rebuke thee.*[1]

> *For the Lord himself shall descend from heaven with a shout, with the voice of the archangel, and with the trump of God: and the dead in Christ shall rise first:*[2]

The word "archangel" in these verses is translated from the Greek word *archaggelos* (ar-khang'-el-os), which has the meaning "chief of the angels."[3] This does not necessarily mean that only one angel is chief but that each archangel is "chief" over his particular host of angels.

The Bible tells us that Lucifer, son of the morning, became filled with pride and iniquity and was cast out of his place in heaven as an archangel.

> *"How you are fallen from heaven, O Lucifer, son of the morning! How you are cut down to the ground, You who weakened the nations! For you have said in your heart:'I will ascend into heaven, I will exalt my throne above the stars of God; I will also sit on the mount of the congregation On the farthest sides of the north; I will ascend above the heights of the clouds, I will be like the Most High.'"*(Isaiah 14:12-14).

This exhibition of pride and iniquity stirred the heavens to warfare and Michael, the archangel, cast Lucifer and all of his host out of the sacred precincts. We find this account recorded in the book of Revelation:

> *His tail drew a third of the stars of heaven and threw them to the earth....And war broke out in heaven: Michael and his angels fought with the dragon; and the dragon and his angels fought, but they did not prevail, nor was a place found for them in heaven any longer....So the great dragon was cast out, that serpent of old, called the Devil and Satan, who deceives the whole world; he was cast to the earth, and his angels were cast out with him* (Revelation 12:4,7-9).

Any time pride and iniquity raises its head in the presence of God and the Church, war takes place. In this war the enemy was cast to the earth with one-third of the angels, those that had been involved in the glory and music of

Any time pride and iniquity raises its head in the presence of God and the Church, war takes place.

heaven. This left only two archangels in heaven, Michael and Gabriel, and two heavenly hosts, the warfare host and the ministering host. These two hosts are left to work for God and to minister among God's people. They remain at work even until this present day.

In Genesis 19, two angels visited Lot in Sodom. One came to warn Lot to get out of the city and protect his family, the other to administer the judgment of God against the sin-filled cities, Sodom and Gomorrah.

Discerning the Spirits of this End Time Apostolic Age

> *Now the two angels came to Sodom in the evening, and Lot was sitting in the gate of Sodom. When Lot saw them, he rose to meet them, and he bowed himself with his face toward the ground. And he said, "Here now, my lords, please turn in to your servant's house and spend the night, and wash your feet; then you may rise early and go on your way." And they said, "No, but we will spend the night in the open square"* (Genesis 19:1-2).

In Genesis 32:1-2, Jacob witnessed these two hosts of angels:

> *And Jacob went on his way, and the angels of God met him. And when Jacob saw them, he said, This is God's host: and he called the name of that place Mahanaim.*[4]

The name "Mahanaim" is translated from the Hebrew word *Machanayim* (makh-an-ah'-yim), which means "two hosts" or "two camps."[5] I believe these angels were both messenger/ministering angels and warrior angels. The ministering angels were there to strengthen Jacob for the wrestling encounter he would have later at Peniel, and the warrior angels were there to stand against Esau if he did not repent and humble his heart in forgiveness towards Jacob. (Remember, Esau came with 400 men to take the revenge he had been waiting for 40 years.) The kind of angel you see may depend on whether you are standing for or against God's chosen ones. We will discuss further the enemy and his fallen host of demonic spirits in chapter three. But for now let's look at Michael and Gabriel. The following passages refer to Michael, the chief warrior angel:

> *At that time Michael shall stand up, the great prince who*

stands watch over the sons of your people; and there shall be a time of trouble, such as never was since there was a nation, even to that time... (Daniel 12:1).

Michael and his host continue to stand watch over the people of God in this very hour. How many times in your life has there been an unexplained delay that prevented you from being in an disastrous situation or an unexplainable event that prevented harm? Jude points out that Michael contends with the enemy whenever he seeks to harass the children of God.....dead or alive.

Yet Michael the archangel, in contending with the devil, when he disputed about the body of Moses, dared not bring against him a reviling accusation, but said, "The Lord rebuke you!" (Jude 1:9).

In Daniel 10, after three weeks of fasting, Daniel was visited by Gabriel the archangel who delivered the revelation of the 70 weeks.

Now on the twenty-fourth day of the first month, as I was by the side of the great river, that is, the Tigris, I lifted my eyes and looked, and behold, a certain man clothed in linen, whose waist was girded with gold of Uphaz! His body was like beryl, his face like the appearance of lightning, his eyes like torches of fire, his arms and feet like burnished bronze in color, and the sound of his words like the voice of a multitude. And I, Daniel, alone saw the vision, for the men who were with me did not see the vision; but a great terror fell upon them, so that they fled to hide themselves.

The fear of God often accompanies ministering angels.

Therefore I was left alone when I saw this great vision, and no strength remained in me; for my vigor was turned to frailty in me, and I retained no strength. Yet I heard the sound of his words; and while I heard the sound of his words I was in a deep sleep on my face, with my face to the ground. Suddenly, a hand touched me, which made me tremble on my knees and on the palms of my hands. And he said to me, "O Daniel, man greatly beloved, understand the words that I speak to you, and stand upright, for I have now been sent to you." While he was speaking this word to me, I stood trembling. Then he said to me, "Do not fear, Daniel, for from the first day that you set your heart to understand, and to humble yourself before your God, your words were heard; and I have come because of your words. "But the prince of the kingdom of Persia withstood me twenty-one days; and behold, Michael, one of the chief princes, came to help me, for I had been left alone there with the kings of Persia. "Now I have come to make you understand what will happen to your people in the latter days, for the vision refers to many days yet to come." (Daniel 10:4-14).

From the first day the revelation was sent by God from heaven through the archangel Gabriel. But the demonic influence of the "prince of Persia" hindered the message from being delivered for three long weeks. Gabriel was not involved nor skilled in the affairs of warfare so he had to wait for the help of Michael, who being skilled in warfare was able to clear the way that the message might be delivered. In Acts 12, Herod begins to persecute the Church and goes as far as

Angelic Spirits

killing James, the brother of John, and throwing Peter in prison:

> *Now about that time Herod the king stretched out his hand to harass some from the church. Then he killed James the brother of John with the sword. And because he*

The judgment wheels of God may grind slowly but they do grind fine.

> *saw that it pleased the Jews, he proceeded further to seize Peter also. Now it was during the Days of Unleavened Bread.* (Acts 12:1-3).

Things looked pretty bleak for the apostles until a warrior angel showed up on the scene:

> *Now behold, an angel of the Lord stood by him, and a light shone in the prison; and he struck Peter on the side and raised him up, saying, "Arise quickly!" And his chains fell off his hands. Then the angel said to him, "Gird yourself and tie on your sandals"; and so he did. And he said to him, "Put on your garment and follow me." So he went out and followed him, and did not know that what was done by the angel was real, but thought he was seeing a vision. When they were past the first and the second guard posts, they came to the iron gate that leads to the city, which opened to them of its own accord; and they went out and went down one street, and immediately the angel departed from him. And when Peter had come to himself, he said, "Now I know for certain that the Lord*

has sent His angel, and has delivered me from the hand of Herod and from all the expectation of the Jewish people" (Acts 12:7-11).

The judgment wheels of God may grind slowly but they do grind fine. Often God uses His host of warrior angels to administer His judgment on those who oppose the advance of His kingdom. As this episode concludes, we find this to be so:

So on a set day Herod, arrayed in royal apparel, sat on his throne and gave an oration to them. And the people kept shouting, "The voice of a god and not of a man!" Then immediately an angel of the Lord struck him, because he did not give glory to God. And he was eaten by worms and died (Acts 12:21-23).

We have witnessed-modern day accounts of the warrior angels of the Lord executing the judgment of God against those who stand against God's children. Brother Teklemariam, the General Superintendent of the Apostolic Church of Ethiopia, shared with me a true account that occurred in the mid 1970's in the country of Ethiopia. He and 150 other pastors had been preaching the revelation of the name of Jesus so strongly that several of the members of the communist government rose up against them. In third world countries, if the leaders of a city or nation do not like you, they just "get rid" of you. They accomplish this through execution. At times, entire tribes or religious groups have been eliminated in this fashion. We in America are often never even aware that such an extermination has taken place. But it only takes a few visits to third world countries to become aware of the kind of terror that occurs.

What follows is a list of some of the genocidal and

religious cleansings that have taken place over the past five decades:

USSR: Stalin's terror, 1936-53, 20 million plus[6,7]
Rwanda: Hutus vs Tutsis, 3 months 1994, 1 million[8] *
   *Other estimates are of 500,000+ deaths
   for this period (*Economist* 8/20/94 pp.33)
Bosnia: "Ethnic cleansing," 1992, 200,000[9]
Eritrea vs Cuba/Ethiopia, 1961-91, 1 million deaths by famine, 1984-85, 2 million[10]
Russia/USSR: 7-12 million civilian deaths by Nazis[11]
Europe: The Holocaust, 1933-45, 6 million[12]
Sino-Japanese War: 1937-45, 3.5 million[13]
Cambodia: Khmer Rouge killing fields, 1975-79, 1.6 million[14]
Afghanistan vs. Soviets, 1979-89, 1.3 million[15]
China: Civil war, 1945-49, 1.2 million[16]
Sudan: Civil war, 1955-72, 1983, (incl. 250,000 famine deaths in 1988) 1 million[17]
Nigeria: Civil war (Biafra), 1967-70, including famine deaths 500,000[18]
Iran-Iraq war, 1987-1992, 500,000[19]
Algeria: FLN vs France, 1954-62, 300,000[20]
Pakistan: Reprisals against Bengalis, 9 months in 1971, 250,000[21]
Indonesia: Civil war, 1965-66, 250,000[22]
Indonesia: Timor war, 1975-88, 200,000[23]
China: Mao's reign of terror, 1949-65, 20 million plus[24]
Kurdistan: Kurds vs Iraq, Iran, Syria, Turkey, 1925, 500,000[25]
Congo: Congo-Kinshasa unrest, 1960-66, 110,000[26]
Rwanda: Hutu massacre of Tutsis, 1956-65, 105,000[27]
Burundi: Tutsi slaughter of Hutus, 1972, 300,000[28]

These kinds of mass killings are inspired and inflamed by demonic spirits. In this episode in Ethiopia, the government had imprisoned the 150 pastors and scheduled then for execution the very next day. Their only crime was that they had preached the name of Jesus. Jesus warned His followers that this kind of persecution that would occur: "And you will be hated by all for My name's sake. But not a hair of your head shall be lost" (Luke 21:17-18). He also told them: "Then they will deliver you up to tribulation and kill you, and you will be hated by all nations for My name's sake" (Matthew 24:9).

The truth of these verses is seen clearly in foreign countries where our missionaries have suffered intense persecution for preaching the revelation of Jesus Christ and the gospel of the death, burial, and resurrection of our Lord and Savior. I will not take the time or space to try to share the dozens of accounts I have heard concerning missionaries around the world and their persecution. It is interesting, however, that the common thread in each story is that in the midst of extreme persecution and suffering there is some kind of special angelic ministry.

The following morning, the community leaders led Brother Teklemariam and the 150 pastors out before a platform. The governor of the region sat on the platform with a scepter in his hand. The area was surrounded by about 20,000 angry villagers standing with stones, lead pipes, machetes, broken bottles, and spears. The atmosphere was highly charged as if a riot was about to break out. The crowd had been incited to anger by the community leaders and further stirred up by demonic spirits. They were anxiously waiting for the governor to stand and raise his golden scepter to pronounce the final judgment upon the pastors. This would release the people to stampede them and kill them.

Brother Teklemariam and the pastors were not weeping or praying for their release, but were actually dancing and rejoicing, crying out with the jubilant anthem, "Maranatha! Thank you, Jesus, that we have the honor of dying as martyrs for your name, just like Peter, James, John, and the disciples!" As they were dancing and rejoicing, the governor attempted to rise from his chair. But push and strain as he might, he could not stand up. The angel of the Lord had him pressed down in the chair. In a desperate effort, he finally pushed himself to his feet whereupon the angel of the Lord proceeded to choked him. The man fell over backwards and died on the spot!

Brother Teklemariam did not realize what was happening as he was dancing and worshiping all over the place with his eyes closed. Suddenly he heard a great commotion and opened his eyes to see what was happening. What he saw was the crowd of people rushing in toward him and the pastors. He closed his eyes again and shouted out, "Thank you, Jesus, for we are coming home!" When he opened his eyes again he was shocked to see that the people had dropped their stones, broken bottles, and other weapons and were skidding toward him on their knees. They then placed his and the pastors' hands on their heads and cried out saying, " We repent! Please pray for us that the angel does not kill us to!"

What a mighty testimony to the ministering spirits of warrior angels. Praise God! When we stand for the name of Jesus, He will stand for us. When we are not ashamed to preach the revelation of His name, He will place us in a special place of protection and angelic intervention. This truth is supported in the book of Proverbs: "The name of the

LORD is a strong tower: the righteous runneth into it, and is safe"[29] (Proverbs 18:10). The word "safe" in this verse is translated from the Hebrew word *sagab* (saw-gab'), which means "to be high, to be inaccessibly high, to be set on high, to be safely set on high."[30]

We can have confidence that when we stand for His name, we will be set on high, out of reach of the enemies attempts to harm us. When we pray the effectual prayers of a righteous church, warrior angelic spirits are released to fight on our behalf in the heavenlies.

As I mentioned earlier, there is something I have been taught to do by my mentors, Brothers Billy Cole and Lee Stoneking. When I fly into different cities or countries of the world, at the moment the wheels of the airplane touch down on the landing strip of that particular city or country I proclaim, "Lord, I enter this city (or country) in your name, Jesus! I serve notice to all spirits and principalities that I come in Jesus' name to conduct warfare through prayer, fasting, and the power of the Word." I believe that when this proclamation of faith is made that thousands of warrior angels that have traveled with me move out across the countryside to effect warfare as I endeavor to do the will of God. Men who have gained great authority in their ministries often have thousands of angels appointed by God traveling with them to work in their behalf.

I realize this may seem "way out there" to some people, and I do not mean to be offensive, but I would not share these principles if I did not believe them with all of my heart. I can testify that I have tried them and proven them to be true.

Angelic Spirits

In the summer of 1991 I was preaching a revival for the esteemed prophet, Brother T.W. Barnes. One morning while praying at the church, Brother Barnes asked me to come into his office. I sat down in a chair and waited for the words of wisdom or prophecy which I felt certain he was about to speak to me. But Brother Barnes just looked across the room silently at me. Suddenly he looked above my head and proclaimed, "Yep, you have hosts of angels residing over your ministry. That's right, the extensive amount of prayer and fasting you have done has caused thousands of angelic spirits to reside over your ministry." He did not offer to explain what he meant and at that time I was too scared to ask him. The next year during another revival he stopped in the aisle and looked at me and said, "Yep, there are more angels."

These statements did not have a lot of impact on me until the summer of 1992. I was about to get married and decided to spend a 14-day period alone in prayer and fasting on a nearby mountain park. As a single young man I cherished these solitary times I spent alone with God. I knew when I was married I would not be able to do this since I would have

Suddenly I became aware that I could hear the sounds of thousands of voices singing up out of the valley in four or five part harmony.

the responsibility of a family. Every day I arose from my campsite at about sunrise, took a long walking stick and several bottles of water, and set out walking down forest trails. I would walk all morning and into the midday simply praying and talking to Jesus. Two or three hours before sunset I would begin to make my way back to my campsite, usually arriving around sunset.

On the ninth day of this fast I set out on a mountain trail and after walking and communing with the Lord for about an hour came to a bend in the trail. About twenty feet from the trail there was a drop off of about 4,000 feet. Standing near the edge I could see the entire valley and forest below, set against the backdrop of distant majestic mountains. The morning fog was just beginning to burn off. This picturesque scene seemed almost heavenly. I was so taken by the beauty that I lifted my hands, closed my eyes, and began to sing one of my favorite worship hymns, "Sing Hallelujah to the Lord." After singing it through several times, I became lost in the spirit of prayer and worship. I then began to do something I had done many times alone in all-night prayer meetings at Life Tabernacle in Houston, Texas. There I would spend hours lying on my back near the altar, praying in tongues and singing this song but letting the words come forth in tongues of the Spirit. (Paul wrote in 1 Corinthians 14:15 that he would "pray with the spirit" and "also pray with the understanding." That he would "sing with the spirit" and "also sing with the understanding.") During these divine sessions of singing in the Spirit I would feel goose bumps on my arms and neck and often feel the hair stand up. I learned to recognize this as one of the signs that angelic spirits were near. This truth is supported in the book of Job: "Then a spirit passed before my face; the hair on my body stood up" (Job 4:15). Psalms 104:4 also records: "Who makes His angels spirits, His ministers a flame of fire."

As I stood there singing this familiar tune in the tongues

Angelic Spirits

of the Spirit I once again began to feel the hair on my arms stand up. Suddenly I became aware that I could hear the sounds of thousands of voices singing up out of the valley in four or five part harmony. The music and singing was more beautiful that any I had heard in my entire life. Initially I was startled and lowered my hands and opened my eyes. When I did this, the singing faded away. I closed my eyes and began to focus my attention again upon worshiping the Lord, singing in tongues. After a while the singing began to float up from the valley before me. I continued to sing with greater fervency and intensity and the singing also increased in volume and intensity until it seemed that I could feel and hear the fluttering of angels' wings all around me. By now I was weeping and trembling in the presence of the Lord and His host. I fell to my knees as such an incredible ministry swept over me.

This went on for what seemed like hours until, like a flash, I realized what was happening. I then fell on my face and began to repent saying, "Oh God, please forgive me for my insensitivity and selfishness these past nine days. I have been on this mountain and these thousands of angels that you have placed over my ministry have been here. Lord, there is a pastor on the east coast that is facing intense warfare in his church. Lord, loose these angels which Brother Barnes declared were over my ministry out to minister in behalf of this pastor. In a moment I knew they were gone. At the end of that period of fasting and prayer, I returned to the church where I had been conducting revival and the secretary handed me a memo. The pastor from the east coast had called and stated that at the exact time I had prayed the prayer (allowing three hours for the time difference), the situation of warfare in his church had broken and the result had been great victory. Now, in every city and country I enter for ministry I pray, "Lord, let the host of angels that Brother Barnes spoke of be loosed across this city to effect warfare as I minister and preach the Word."

Soon after the angelic visitation on the mountainside in 1992, the Lord revealed this portion of Scripture to me:

And they came over unto the other side of the sea, into the country of the Gadarenes. And when he was come out of the ship, immediately there met him out of the tombs a man with an unclean spirit, who had his dwelling among the tombs; and no man could bind him, no, not with chains: Because that he had been often bound with fetters and chains, and the chains had been plucked asunder by him, and the fetters broken in pieces: neither could any man tame him. And always, night and day, he was in the mountains, and in the tombs, crying, and cutting himself with stones. But when he saw Jesus afar off, he ran and worshiped him, And cried with a loud voice, and said, What have I to do with thee, Jesus, thou Son of the most high God? I adjure thee by God, that thou torment me not. For he said unto him, Come out of the man, thou unclean spirit. And he asked him, What is thy name? And he answered, saying, My name is Legion: for we are many.[31] (Mark 5:19)

The word "legion" in this verse is translated from the Latin *legeon* (leg-eh-ohn'), which means a body of soldiers whose number differed at different times, and in the time of Augustus seems to have consisted of 6826 men (i.e. 6100 foot soldiers, and 726 horsemen)[32] The Lord impressed upon me the thought that if one man could live so wickedly that he

Angelic Spirits

ended up being possessed by over 6,000 spirits of fallen angels, then why couldn't one man fast, pray, and live a life so governed by the Word and Spirit of God that thousands of angels would become be drawn to his side to serve as his legion of holy soldiers.

Another account of the warrior angels of the Lord standing for the children of God can be found in 2 Chronicles 20. In response to the obedience of King Jehoshaphat and the people of Judah to the prophetic word given by the prophet Jahaziel and in response to their unity in worship and praise, the Lord sets a host of warrior angels against the children of Moab, Ammon, and Mount Seir. The Bible says:

And when he had consulted with the people, he appointed those who should sing to the Lord, and who should praise the beauty of holiness, as they went out before the army and were saying: "Praise the Lord, for His mercy endures forever." Now when they began to sing and to praise, the Lord set ambushes against the people of Ammon, Moab, and Mount Seir, who had come against Judah; and they were defeated (2 Chronicles 20:21-22).

These ambushes were none other than the angels of the Lord that encamp around those who fear Him.

The Old and New Testaments record at least 42 accounts of Michael and his host standing for the children of God to do warfare and Gabriel and his host ministering for the children of God. God is not going to minister to His people through His hosts for 5,000 years and then suddenly change His mind and stop this principle of ministry. This kind of ministry continues in our day.

We have discussed Michael the warrior archangel and his

host; so let us now discuss Gabriel, the messenger archangel, and his host. The first emergence of Gabriel delivering a revelation from God in the Scriptures can be found in the book of Daniel:

Then it happened, when I, Daniel, had seen the vision and was seeking the meaning, that suddenly there stood before me one having the appearance of a man. And I heard a man's voice between the banks of the Ulai, who called, and said, "Gabriel, make this man understand the vision." So he came near where I stood, and when he came I was afraid and fell on my face; but he said to me, "Understand, son of man, that the vision refers to the time of the end" (Daniel 8:15-17).

It is interesting to note that this angelic intervention occurred while Daniel was searching for an understanding of

Angelic visitations are usually divine interventions into our normal every-day lives.

the vision he had received from God. Daniel was not on an "angel hunt." Most people I have spoken to who have experienced an angelic visitation had their experience during the process of either seeking the face of God in prayer or during an attempt to fulfill the will of God. Angelic visitations are usually divine interventions into our normal every-day lives. The visitation or ministry usually occurs so quickly and unexpectedly that it is over and past before we even realize that it was a divine ministry or intervention.

Most Bible scholars have recognized Gabriel as a

Angelic Spirits

messenger or ministering archangel. Throughout the Bible, Gabriel and his host are most often found delivering a message or revelation to the people of God. A good example can be found in Daniel 10:

Yes, while I was speaking in prayer, the man Gabriel, whom I had seen in the vision at the beginning, being caused to fly swiftly, reached me about the time of the evening offering. And he informed me, and talked with me, and said, "O Daniel, I have now come forth to give you skill to understand. At the beginning of your supplications the command went out, and I have come to tell you, for you are greatly beloved; therefore consider the matter, and understand the vision" (Daniel 10:21-23).

It is interesting to note that Gabriel held the power and authority to *give* divine revelation and understanding concerning the secrets of God. If we would understand and receive this truth into our lives, then whenever we need greater understanding or revelation of the things of the Spirit we will simply pray for the Lord to release Gabriel and the ministering host to release this into our minds. Go ahead, try it now. Bow your head and ask God to release His ministering host into the situation in your life where you need greater revelation. Now don't expect a ten foot angel to come walking into your room this instant. In fact, this may never happen. To my knowledge I have never had a ten foot angel visit me.

Most things of the Spirit occur as a result of faith. Hebrews 11:1 says: "Now faith is the substance of things hoped for, the evidence of things not seen."

Many times I have been praying for understanding about a

certain situation and suddenly I sensed that someone had entered the room. The atmosphere of the spirit realm had "changed." Often the hair on the back of my neck and arms has suddenly stood up. Though I could see nothing in the natural realm, I sensed by faith what was occurring. Then revelation began to flow into me like a bright shining light. This has occurred while I lying on the church auditorium floor with my Bible opened before me. As a matter of fact, I feel it right now as I sit on this airplane! Isn't that incredible? Faith is what brings these angelic ministrations of revelation and understanding to us no matter what the setting may be.

I mentioned before that Michael and his host are primarily set to minister in judgment and warfare while Gabriel and his host are primarily set to minister as messengers and ministering angels. While this stands true throughout the Scriptures, this does not exclude Gabriel from administering judgment. The passage found in Luke 1 seems to suggest that at the time Gabriel was delivering the divine message he was also involved in administering judgment in response to Zacharias' unbelief.

> *And the angel answered and said to him, "I am Gabriel, who stands in the presence of God, and was sent to speak to you and bring you these glad tidings. "But behold, you will be mute and not able to speak until the day these things take place, because you did not believe my words which will be fulfilled in their own time"* (Luke 1:19-20).

I have found it a safe practice not to establish absolutes concerning what goes on in the spirit realm. It seems that as soon as we think we have it "all figured out" and have become an "authority" on some principle of the spirit realm,

Angelic Spirits

an new experience or some further revelation through the Word of God sends us back to the proverbial "drawing board." Oh, how many times have I had the opportunity to sit down and listen to a tape of myself preaching eight or ten years ago and cringe as I heard my self emphatically preaching with great enthusiasm and "authority" a principle of the spirit realm which I now know I did not understand in the fullness of revelation. Or how many books have I gone back and revised on the second or third printing because of a greater understanding of some truth I had written about.

I recall an amusing story (which was not so amusing at the time it occurred) that happened at a conference where I was speaking. I had just finished preaching a message on "spiritual authority" in which I had used an illustration from Luke 8:26-32. The demons that possessed the man from the country of the Gadarenes were beseeching Jesus that he would not command them to go out into the deep. I showed that the word "deep" was the same Greek word used for the words "bottomless pit" found in the book of Revelation (20:1-3). In these verses the angel that held the key to the bottomless pit bound the enemy with a chain and cast him into the pit for a thousand years. Both words "deep" and "pit" in these verses were translations of the Greek word *abussos* (ab'-us-sos), which means a bottomless pit, deep, or the immeasurable depth.[33] I then proceeded to make a "quantum leap" and say, "Therefore, when we pray for demons to be bound and cast out, don't just cast them out and leave them where they can torment others again; cast them into the deep or the pit where they can never torment again."

The response from the one thousand plus people was incredible. They shouted and clapped their hands with fervency. When I finished this time of ministry and took my seat, I was followed by one of our patriarchs of the gospel. This elder proceeded to make the statement in front of the entire crowd, "I really don't know where that young man got this nonsense about casting spirit's into the deep, but if you try that, they won't go very far."

I now simply teach the authority of the church over demonic forces in this hour through prayer, fasting, and faith in the Word of God, leaving the "pit casting" up to Michael and his host. Needless to say, I felt like crawling under the pew and vanishing. I still make a few leaps now and then, but I precede them with "there is a possibility." I certainly learned my lesson that day.

The possibility of Michael being involved in ministry and the delivering of divine messages and Gabriel being involved in the administering of judgement and warfare are suggested in the Scriptures, though I am personally convinced that their primary roles are as previously explained.

One final scriptural reference on Gabriel is the prophetic account recorded in 1 Thessalonians 4:16: "For the Lord Himself will descend from heaven with a shout, with the voice of an archangel, and with the trumpet of God. And the dead in Christ will rise first." It will be the archangel Gabriel that will deliver the final message of the coming of the Lord with a loud voice and the blowing of the trumpet of God. One final message that Gabriel and his host will deliver will be the announcement of the coming of the Lord.

We will take only a brief look at Lucifer, the third archangel, since we will be further discussing him in Chapter 3. Scriptural references found in Isaiah 14:12, Luke 10:18, Luke 1:21-22, Revelation 12:1-12, all refer to the falling, stripping, and demise of this fallen archangel. Lucifer was over the glory and music of heaven and walked in the midst

Angelic Spirits

of the stones of fire (Ezekiel 28:13-19). We should note that this fallen archangel is fallen from the fire of God's presence. With the war in heaven, one-third of the stars or angels which were under Lucifer fell to the earth. This brings us to the next chapter, which deals with fallen angels or demonic spirits.

Endnotes for Chapter 2:

1. *The King James Version*, (Cambridge: Cambridge, 1769).

2. Ibid.

3. *Enhanced Strong's Lexicon*, (Oak Harbor, WA: Logos Research Systems, Inc., 1995).

4. *The King James Version*, (Cambridge: Cambridge) 1769.

5. *Enhanced Strong's Lexicon*, (Oak Harbor, WA: Logos Research Systems, Inc., 1995).

6. Charny, *Genocide: a critical bibliographic review*, (1988), Vol.2, pp.87

7. Matthews, *Guiness Book of Records*, (1994), pp.184-85.

8. Masland, "Will it be Peace or Punishment?," *Newsweek*, (August 1, 1994), pp.37.

9. Ibid.

10. Clodfelter, *Warfare and Armed Conflicts*, (1992), Vol. 2., pp.22

11. Ibid.

12. Ibid.

13. Ibid.

14. Ibid.

15. Ibid.

16. Ibid.

17. Ibid.

18. Ibid.

19. Ibid.

20. Ibid.

21. Ibid.

22. Ibid.

23. Ibid.

24. Elliot, *Twentieth Century Book of the Dead*, (1972), pp.77

25. "Estmated War Casualties" (Table), *Cultural Survival Quarterly*, 11(3):11.

26. Bouthoul, "A list of the 366 Majot Armed Conflicts of the period 1740-1974," *Peace Research*, (1978) 10(3):83-108.

27. Ibid.

28. "Burundi: Not a Twin," *Economist*, (August 20, 1994), pp.34.

29. *The King James Version*, (Cambridge: Cambridge,1769).

30. *Enhanced Strong's Lexicon*, (Oak Harbor, WA: Logos Research Systems, Inc., 1995).

31. *The King James Version*, (Cambridge: Cambridge, 1769).

32. *Enhanced Strong's Lexicon*, (Oak Harbor, WA: Logos Research Systems, Inc., 1995).

33. Ibid.

3

Demonic Spirits

Before we discuss anything about demonic spirits, we will first deal with the past status, present condition, and future dilemma of the enemy. No matter how highly the enemy may try to exalt himself, remember, he is fallen, stripped, and broken. Even in his greatest strength and numbers, there are still two angels for every demonic spirit.

As I have stated, in the beginning there were three angelic hosts, each led by a different archangel. These archangels and hosts were: Michael, the archangel set over the warfare matters of the kingdom of God; Gabriel, the archangel set over the messenger, ministering, and harvesting angels; and Lucifer, son of the morning, set over the glory and music of the kingdom of God.

We understand from Isaiah 14:12-14 that Lucifer became

filled with pride and iniquity and was cast out of his place in heaven as an archangel.

> *How you are fallen from heaven, O Lucifer, son of the morning! How you are cut down to the ground, you who weakened the nations! For you have said in your heart: 'I will ascend into heaven, I will exalt my throne above the stars of God; I will also sit on the mount of the congregation on the farthest sides of the north; I will ascend above the heights of the clouds, I will be like the Most High.'*

This exhibition of pride and iniquity moved the heavens to warfare, and the archangel Michael cast Lucifer out with all his host. We find this account recorded in Revelation 12:7-11:

> *And war broke out in heaven: Michael and his angels fought with the dragon; and the dragon and his angels fought, but they did not prevail, nor was a place found for them in heaven any longer. So the great dragon was cast out, that serpent of old, called the Devil and Satan, who deceives the whole world; he was cast to the earth, and his angels were cast out with him.*

In this war the enemy was cast to the earth along with one-third of the angels of heaven that were involved in the glory and music of heaven. This is where demonic spirits originated.

> *His tail drew a third of the stars of heaven and threw them to the earth. And the dragon stood before the woman who was ready to give birth, to devour her Child as soon*

> *The adversary's future is that he be bound for one thousand years and ultimately cast into the lake of fire.*

as it was born (Revelation 12:4).

As recorded in Isaiah 14:12-14, the enemy's fall started when he desired preeminence above his fellow archangels ("I will exalt myself among the stars") and ended when he considered himself equal with God. In these three verses alone the enemy says "I will" five times. This was a blatant presentation of iniquity in the midst of the fire and Shekinah Glory of God. We find this fall further recorded in Ezekiel 28:13-17:

> *You were in Eden, the garden of God; every precious stone was your covering: the sardius, topaz, and diamond, beryl, onyx, and jasper, sapphire, turquoise, and emerald with gold. The workmanship of your timbrels and pipes was prepared for you on the day you were created. "You were the anointed cherub who covers; I established you; you were on the holy mountain of God; you walked back and forth in the midst of fiery stones. You were perfect in your ways from the day you were created,* **till iniquity was found in you.** *By the abundance of your trading you became filled with violence within, and you sinned; Therefore I cast you as a profane thing out of the mountain of God; and I destroyed you, O*

covering cherub, from the midst of the fiery stones. Your heart was lifted up because of your beauty; you corrupted your wisdom for the sake of your splendor; I cast you to the ground, I laid you before kings that they might gaze at you.

We must not hold an irrational fear of the enemy. The adversary has fallen from his original position of authority because of his iniquity. The opposition is presently limited to time and territory. Only the one true God is omniscient (all knowing), omnipotent (all powerful), and omnipresent (everywhere in time or territory). The enemy is limited to the geographical territory under his authority. When the church destroys his strongholds through prayer, fasting, and the preaching of the Word, his works are brought to naught. (I cover this in more detail in my book *Three Warfare's*). The adversary's future is that he be bound for one thousand years and ultimately cast into the lake of fire.

Then I saw an angel coming down from heaven, having the key to the bottomless pit and a great chain in his hand. He laid hold of the dragon, that serpent of old, who is the Devil and Satan, and bound him for a thousand years; and he cast him into the bottomless pit, and shut him up, and set a seal on him, so that he should deceive the nations no more till the thousand years were finished. But after these things he must be released for a little while (Revelation 20:1-2).

Demonic Spirits

Notice in the first verse of this passage the authority the host of God has over the enemy. It will only take one angel to bind the enemy and cast him into the bottomless pit for a thousand years. Revelation 20:7 and 10 continues to expose his future:

Now when the thousand years have expired, Satan will be released from his prison ... the devil, who deceived them, was cast into the lake of fire and brimstone where the beast and the false prophet are. And they will be tormented day and night forever and ever.

The enemy knows that his time is short and that all he has to look forward to is eternal torment, day and night, forever and ever. The next time he tries to condemn you for your past failures, *remind him that he couldn't even serve God when there was no sin and no devil!* It is he who is the loser. He has no hope for mercy. The fate of the enemy and his host is sealed.

> *The next time he tries to condemn you for your past failures, remind him that he couldn't even serve God when there was no sin and no devil!.*

God will have mercy on sin or human failure as long as there is genuine repentance and a turning away from sin. God's dealings with man has always been conditional—"If you will do.....then I will do." For example, *"If we confess our sins*, he is faithful and just to forgive us our sins, and to cleanse us from all unrighteousness" (1 John 1:9). [i] *"If My people* who are called by My name will humble themselves, and pray and seek My face, and turn from their wicked ways, *then I will* hear from heaven, and will forgive their sin and heal their land (2 Chronicles 7:14). "Behold, I stand at the door and knock. *If anyone hears* My voice and opens the

> *To the contrary, iniquity (self-will), which was the original sin, angers God.*

door, *I will come* in to him and dine with him, and he with Me. To him who overcomes I will grant to sit with Me on My throne, as I also overcame and sat down with My Father on His throne" (Revelation 3:20-21).

Yes, God does have a conditional working relationship with mankind as long as man will humble himself, turn from sin, and pray, seeking the face of God. To the contrary, iniquity (self-will), which was the original sin, angers God. When one has the attitude, "I don't care what the Bible says" or "It doesn't matter what God thinks, I will live my life as I please," this can bring the judgment of God. If only the world would bow their hearts to God's commandments, then hell would only contain what it was originally prepared for: the enemy and the host of fallen angels. As Jesus said, "Then He will also say to those on the left hand, 'Depart from Me, you cursed, into the everlasting fire *prepared for the devil and his angels'"* (Matthew 25:41). The first record of demons and their influence is found in Genesis 1:1-3:

> *In the beginning God created the heaven and the earth. And the earth was without form, and void; and darkness was upon the face of the deep. And the Spirit of God moved upon the face of the waters. And God said, Let there be light: and there was light.*[ii]

The word "darkness" in Verse 2 is translated from the Hebrew word *choshek* (kho-shek'), which in different forms has the meanings, misery, destruction, death, sorrow, wickedness.[iii] This list sounds much like what the enemy leaves behind when he has been around. I believe this darkness was all of the forces of fallen angels that had fallen from heaven to earth. Nevertheless, notice how all the forces of hell covering the face of the deep could not keep the Spirit of God from moving on the face of the waters. No matter how dark it may get in your life, be assured that God is still moving and working in the midst of your darkest hour. Jesus recounted the fall of the enemy in Luke 10:17-19:

> *Then the seventy returned with joy, saying, "Lord, even the demons are subject to us in Your name." And He said to them, "**I saw Satan fall like lightning from heaven**. Behold, I give you the authority to trample on serpents and scorpions, and over all the power of the enemy, and nothing shall by any means hurt you."*

Lightning moves at the speed of 186,000 miles per second. Now that is moving! When the enemy and his host were cast out of heaven, they fell to earth at the speed of light!!! When the Lord spoke the word and cast the enemy out of heaven, it did not take a year, a month, a week, a day, or even an hour. In a moment when the word went forth, the enemy was cast out of heaven. It is the same when God speaks His word of hope and deliverance into your situation. In a moment, the enemy must flee! In a moment the chains

> ## *The light of God rides on the wings of His word.*

will be broken and the yoke destroyed. In Genesis 1:3, when God said, "Let there be light," this was not the light from the sun, moon, or stars, as they were not spoken into existence until Genesis 1:14-16.

This light was the light of God which is released by the spoken word. As David wrote in Psalms 119:130, "The entrance of Your words gives light; it gives understanding to the simple."

The light of God rides on the wings of His Word. The Spirit of God moving on the face of the water prepared for what His word would produce. Likewise, the Spirit of God prepares us for what His word produces in our lives.

When time began, darkness did not exist. There was only the light of the Shekinah Glory of God. When the fallen one was cast out of the presence of God with one-third of the host of heaven, darkness became. Darkness is merely the absence of light. Light shines into darkness to penetrate its boundaries. On the contrary, darkness cannot penetrate the borders of light. When light comes, darkness flees. Darkness has no power over light. Darkness has no power at all. Light, on the other hand, is full of energy. Darkness is emptiness, void. Darkness is nothingness. Darkness cannot have its way in your life, family, or city as long as the minutest bit of light is present.

Scientists say that the unassisted human eye can see a single candle from 30 miles away on a clear, dark night. The minutest bit of light can penetrate the densest darkness to bring forth illumination. This is why the enemy hates truth. The truth of the Word of God shines forth light to reveal the works of darkness. In Ephesians 5:11-14 Paul wrote:

And have no fellowship with the unfruitful works of darkness, but rather expose them. For it is shameful even to speak of those things which are done by them in secret. ***But all things that are exposed are made manifest by the light, for whatever makes manifest is light.*** *Therefore He says: "Awake, you who sleep, Arise from the dead, and Christ will give you light."*

So many people choose to repeat the words of darkness and discouragement that the enemy speaks to them. For example, when they are laid off from their job, the enemy tells them, "You are ruined. Your family is going to go without food or clothes. You will lose your house." By the time they get home they are repeating these words of discouragement, defeat, and destruction to the wife and family. When they do this they release sickness, destruction, and death to work in their lives. What this person should say is, "God, you are Jehovah-Jireh, my provider. Reveal your

miraculous provision in my life." Or, "God, every miracle needs an
impossibility. You said you would supply all our needs according to your riches in glory. Show me the miracle of provision."

> ***We must choose to speak forth the words from God that release light, life, blessing, and healing.***

We must choose to speak forth the words from God that release light, life, blessing, and healing. This is what Paul meant when he wrote in Ephesians 5:8, "For you were once darkness, but now you are light in the Lord. Walk as children of light."

When the darkness of discouragement comes and we chose to speak forth, "Though he slay me yet will I trust him," light comes. When the darkness of financial trouble comes into our lives speaking words of failure and defeat, we must choose to speak forth, "I have been young, and now am old; yet I have not seen the righteous forsaken, nor his descendants begging bread" (Psalms 37:25).

Jesus used the Word of God to shine forth the overcoming light in the three temptations recorded in Matthew 4, repeating, "It is written" four times. We also can use the Word to release the overcoming light of God into our troubles and trials. This is why it is so important to hide the Word of God in our hearts. David wrote in Psalms 119:133, "Direct my steps by Your word, and let no iniquity have dominion over me."

Demonic Spirits

The enemy is fallen and stripped of his original power and protection. When you release the Word of God against his darkness, he is cast out by the *finger of God*. I like to think it only takes the pinky to cast him out. "But if I cast out demons with the finger of God, surely the kingdom of God has come upon you. When a strong man, fully armed, guards his own

---

The only power the enemy can have in you, your family, or your city is what you and the church body allow him to have.

---

palace, his goods are in peace. But when a stronger than he comes upon him and overcomes him, he takes from him all his armor in which he trusted, and divides his spoils" (Luke 11:20-22).

The strong man fully armed was the enemy before the Fall and Calvary. With the Fall he was overcome or cast out. With the blood Jesus shed on Calvary he was stripped of all his armor (darkness, lies, possession of mankind), and his spoils (the souls of men) became divided. Every day, more and more are being delivered from the authority of his darkness and delivered into the kingdom of God through the power of the death, burial, and resurrection of Jesus Christ. The only power the enemy can have in you, your family, or your city is what you and the church body allow him to have. John wrote in 1 John 4:4, "You are of God, little children, and have overcome them, because He who is in you is greater than he who is in the world."

When a church sits back in complacency and doesn't

pray, fast, or evangelize with the light of God's Word, the authority of the enemy increases in that city. Similarly, when a body of believers goes aggressively forth in taking authority over principalities and powers through intercessory prayer, extended fasting, and the evangelism of the gospel, the authority of the enemy is greatly diminished in that city. I have observed this principle to be true in every city I have ministered in around the world.

The New Testament believer does not have to live in fear or bondage of the enemy. If he will submit his life to God through His Word, the authority of the enemy is broken from his life. Understanding this, the believer can accurately discern demonic spirits of this age and defeat them without getting off on some wild tangent. The enemy has fallen, is fallen, and will fall even further in the last day.

In Chapter 1, I stated that it is up to the believer to exercise his senses to a keen edge in discerning of spirits. The key word here is "exercise." It takes time to develop the perceptive edge of sensitivity in our spirit man to accurately discern and defeat demonic spirits. Our spiritual senses are much like our natural senses in that once we have learned or experienced a sensation such as smell, that experience becomes indelibly ingrained into our memory. For example, the first time we experience the smell of cooking bacon and see it in the frying pan, our memory registers the smell of bacon with our visual confirmation of what bacon looks like. From that day forward, all we have to do is pick up by our sense of smell the aroma of bacon frying and the mental image of what is cooking allows us to correctly identify that bacon is being cooked. It is not necessary that we have the visual confirmation; we "know" as a result of our sense of smell.

Demonic Spirits

In the same manner, if a parent commits the sin of adultery and introduces that spirit into the home life, the child or spouse becomes very sensitive to the discernment of that spirit in the future. He or she does not need to have physical evidence to support what they sense in the spirit. The more warfare we wage against the spirits of this age, the more sensitive we become to discerning those spirits.

Since the enemy is a master of disguises and deceit, it is vital for all New Testament believers to be sensitive in the gift of discerning of spirits. As Paul tells us, "Satan himself transforms himself into an angel of light. Therefore it is no great thing if his ministers also transform themselves into ministers of righteousness, whose end will be according to their works" (2 Corinthians 11:14-15).

The enemy formerly dwelled in the shekinah fire and holiness of God.(Ezekiel 28:14-17). He was thoroughly schooled in righteousness, but has now plunged into the depths of wickedness. The fallen one knows how to make evil appear good and good appear evil.

Most operations of demonic spirits work in areas of deception and ignorance. Many Christians live bound by fear of the enemy because of deception or ignorance. For instance, the enemy can accurately know events concerning the past and present. He has had over 6,000 years to gain a vast knowledge in the workings of mankind. But he cannot know any event the future holds. Only God knows the future.

In this hour there are those who go to psychics, palm readers, and mediums, thinking that such people can foretell the future. But this is nothing more than ignorance and deception at work and is presently a billion-dollar industry.

Discerning the Spirits of this End Time Apostolic Age

We all have what is called a "familiar spirit" that trails us from birth. This spirit knows intimate details about our life history and character that only we and God know. The duty of this familiar spirit is to attempt to destroy our lives through

All born-again believers are protected by a threefold protection:

alcohol, drugs, or other addictions. He also works through spirits of bondage, suicide, or even murder. If a person never experiences the new birth of water and the Spirit, the authority of this familiar spirit will never be broken.

If a person does repent and get water baptized in the name of Jesus, and receive the gift of the Holy Ghost evidenced by speaking in other tongues, then the authority of this familiar spirit will be broken. All born-again believers are protected by a threefold protection: first, the blood that Jesus shed at Calvary covers our soul; second, the indwelling presence of the Holy Spirit protects our spirit; and finally, the familiar spirit is replaced with the angel of the Lord from that day forward. "The angel of the Lord encamps all around those who fear Him, and delivers them" (Psalms 34:7). A person whose life is not under the authority and protection of the blood of Jesus, the indwelling presence of the Holy Spirit, and angelic protection is wide open for the deception of psychics.

Psychics, mediums, and palm readers are nothing more than deceived persons meddling in witchcraft, necromancy, and the like. Many are probably demonically possessed. When a person allows a psychic to foretell his future, this is

Demonic Spirits

what is really happening at that moment: the psychic (who is either channeling a demonic spirit or is demonically possessed) becomes a vessel for the familiar spirit of the person wanting his future told to speak through. This familiar spirit will then speak through the psychic and tell the person intimate details of his past that no one else could possibly know. This can be so convincing that all doubt and skepticism are put aside. The psychic then tells the person some nonsense about a "vacation in the Bahamas" or a "great financial opportunity opening up" or "the love of their life coming" and the person believes it.

People pay a lot of money for this nonsense. But it is really nothing more than foolishness, deception, enchantments, divination, and *consulting with familiar spirits*. This is also very dangerous as a person could become oppressed or even possessed by entertaining these demonic spirits. This also includes horoscopes (observing times), tarot cards, coffee ground and tea leaves reading (divination), crystal balls, cup reading, needle on pulse reading, pendulum reading, Ouija boards, games that deal with sorcery, etc. We do not need any of that. In fact, we don't need to know the future. We only need to know the One who does!

New Testament believers should never even play in these areas, even out of curiosity. The Lord clearly condemns all such practices:

> *There shall not be found among you any one that maketh his son or his daughter to pass through the fire, or that useth divination, or an observer of times, or an enchanter, or a witch, or a charmer, or a consulter with familiar spirits, or a wizard, or a necromancer* (Deuteronomy 18:10-11)[iv]

The term "familiar spirits" in Verse 11 is translated from the Hebrew word *Õowb* (obe), which means a necromancer or one who evokes the spirit of a dead one.[v] This does not mean that there are human spirits that can remain in contact with those in this life after death. It is the familiar spirit of the dead one that remains behind. We see this illustrated in the account of the dead prophet Samuel and the witch of Endor in 1 Samuel 28:7-19:

Then said Saul unto his servants, "Seek me a woman that hath a familiar spirit, that I may go to her, and enquire of her." And his servants said to him, "Behold, there is a woman that hath a familiar spirit at Endor." And Saul disguised himself, and put on other raiment, and he went, and two men with him, and they came to the woman by night: and he said, "I pray thee, divine unto me by the familiar spirit, and bring me him up, whom I shall name unto thee." And the woman said unto him, "Behold, thou knowest what Saul hath done, how he hath cut off those that have familiar spirits, and the wizards, out of the land: wherefore then layest thou a snare for my life, to cause me to die?" And Saul sware to her by the LORD, saying, "As the LORD liveth, there shall no punishment happen to thee for this thing." Then said the woman, "Whom shall I bring up unto thee?" And he said, "Bring me up Samuel." And when the woman saw Samuel, she cried with a loud voice: and the woman spake to Saul, saying, "Why hast thou deceived me? for thou art Saul." And the king said unto her, "Be not afraid: for what sawest thou?" And the woman said unto Saul, "I saw gods ascending out of the earth." And he said unto her,

Demonic Spirits

"What form is he of?" And she said, "An old man cometh up; and he is covered with a mantle." And Saul perceived that it was Samuel, and he stooped with his face to the ground, and bowed himself. And Samuel said to Saul, "Why hast thou disquieted me, to bring me up?" And Saul answered, "I am sore distressed; for the Philistines make war against me, and God is departed from me, and answereth me no more, neither by prophets [Heb. by the hand of prophets], *nor by dreams: therefore I have called thee, that thou mayest make known unto me what I shall do." Then said Samuel, "Wherefore then dost thou ask of me, seeing the LORD is departed from thee, and is become thine enemy? And the LORD hath done to him, as he spake* [to him or for himself] *by me: for the LORD hath rent the kingdom out of thine hand, and given it to*

> **She replied, "I am part of a local witches coven and I have been sent to tell you that we are praying and fasting that you will fall into sin."**

thy neighbour, even to David: Because thou obeyedst not the voice of the LORD, nor executedst his fierce wrath upon Amalek, therefore hath the LORD done this thing unto thee this day. Moreover the LORD will also deliver Israel with thee into the hand of the Philistines: and to morrow shalt thou and thy sons be with me: the LORD also shall deliver the host of Israel into the hand of the Philistines."[vi]

The first thing we see in Verses 7 and 8 is that Saul seeks out a witch that has a "familiar spirit." In Verse 11, Saul asks the witch to bring up Samuel. The Scriptures never record that King Saul ever saw Samuel, it was the witch who saw the visage. She describes what she saw as "gods ascending out of the earth." I believe the witch had entered a channel of the spirit realm where she was seeing demonic spirit activity. She describes what she saw as "gods" with a small "g." I can't believe that God would allow his deceased prophets, already in paradise, to be harassed at will by a witch. It was therefore the familiar spirit of the deceased prophet Samuel that began to speak to Saul as though it were Samuel himself speaking. Saul, who by now was pulled into the demonic visitation, believed it was Samuel speaking to him. The familiar spirit finally reveals its identity in Verse 19 when it says, "And to morrow shalt thou and thy sons be with me." Saul, who lived his life in self will and rebellion against God, did not go to paradise where Samuel was, but to Hades where the demonic spirit would torment him.

I am convinced that a child of God should immerse himself in the work of the Lord. He should not get involved with "picking fights with the enemy" or become overly interested in being able to discern demonic spirits. Only when the enemy gets so bold as to openly attack a believer should he engage him in a fight. The enemy hates to be ignored. Even though we are involved daily in the war of principalities and powers, our greatest efforts must be toward advancing the kingdom of God, not demonic "search and destroy" missions.

The summer of 1987 was one of the few times I was openly and aggressively attacked by the enemy. I was living in a low income apartment complex as a single young man. For several months I had been aggressively evangelizing the area, teaching many Bible studies. The apartment next to mine had been vacant for several months. Late one night as I was returning from a Bible study, I noticed someone had moved into this apartment. The next evening as I was returning home from work, I saw a lady sitting on the top of the steps leading to both apartments. As I was ascending the stairs I started to greet my new neighbor and tell her my name when she interrupted me and said, "We know who you are, John." This surprised me, so I asked her who "we" was. She replied, "I am part of a local witches coven and I have been sent to tell you that we are praying and fasting that you will fall into sin." I was so shocked that I didn't know what to say. I walked silently past her and entered my apartment.

> **The way to resist the devil is to first submit your life to God.**

For the next three months I woke up many nights at two or three in the morning feeling as though I was suffocating. When I would walk out on my balcony to get some fresh air, I would see the witch's living room completely lit up with well over a hundred candles. There were many other things that happened which would not be edifying so I will refrain from telling about them. My pastor, Brother James Kilgore finally counseled me and said, "This witch is just trying to wear you down. Don't get into a prolonged fight, just move to another apartment across town." I did just that and was able to successfully continue my evangelism without any further attacks from this coven.

James wrote in his epistle: "Therefore submit to God. Resist the devil and he will flee from you. Draw near to God and He will draw near to you. Cleanse your hands, you sinners; and purify your hearts, you double-minded" (James 4:7-8). The way to resist the devil is to first submit your life to God. Then submit your life in obedience to the Word of God. Then draw near to God through prayer, fasting, and daily walking with Him. Immerse yourself in the vision and burden of the Lord for this last hour, ignoring the enemy's plots and traps. And finally, only step into warfare if the enemy challenges you or hinders the work of God from going forward. This is the best way to deal with the fallen, broken demonic spirits.

Endnotes for Chapter 3:

i. *The King James Version*, (Cambridge: Cambridge,1769).

ii. Ibid.

iii. *Enhanced Strong's Lexicon*, (Oak Harbor, WA: Logos Research Systems, Inc., 1995).

iv. The King James Version, (Cambridge: Cambridge) 1769.

v. Enhanced Strong's Lexicon, (Oak Harbor, WA: Logos Research Systems, Inc.) 1995.

vi. The King James Version, (Cambridge: Cambridge) 1769.

Discerning the Spirits of this End Time Apostolic Age

4

The Human Spirit

As I stated in Chapter 1, the two spirits that are the most difficult to differentiate between are the human spirit and the Holy Spirit. The voice of the human spirit and voice of the Holy Spirit are separated by a very thin line. In time, all of us can learn to discern the voices of angels, demons, and the spirits of this age. Yet, the toughest will be discerning the difference between the spirit of man and the Spirit of God. Our human spirit may even use King James English to try to establish authority. How many times have we heard a message in tongues that was from the human spirit prefaced by "Thus saith the Lord"?

The surest and most basic way of becoming skilled at distinguishing between the human spirit and the Spirit of God is by gaining a working knowledge of the written Word. This is one of the most powerful weapons the Lord has given the church. In Matthew 4:1-10, when Jesus was being tempted by the enemy, He used this powerful weapon to defeat him. Three times He responded to the devil's temptations with the words, "It is written" (see *Three Warfare's* by John Arcovio). Paul brought this out in his letter to the Hebrews:

> *For the word of God is quick, and powerful, and sharper than any two-edged sword, piercing even to the dividing asunder of soul and spirit, and of the joints and marrow, and is a discerner of the thoughts and intents of the heart* (Hebrews 4:12).[i]

The word "soul" in this verse is translated from the Greek word *psuche* (psoo-khay'), which means "life, affections, desires, mind, conscience, heart, or the breath of life."[ii] The word "spirit" is translated from the Greek word *pneuma* (pnyoo'-mah), which is widely accepted as referring to the Holy Ghost or the Spirit of God.[iii]
It is the written Word that determines the "dividing asunder" or "distinction" between the human spirit and the Spirit of God.

The inner life of a Christian is often a strange admixture of motivations, some genuinely spiritual and others completely human. To sort these out and expose what is of the Spirit and what is of the flesh requires a supernatural discerning agent such as the Word of God. If a person will saturate his mind and spirit (soul) with the Word of God on a daily basis, he will greatly increase his ability to distinguish the difference between the human spirit and the Spirit of God.

The Human Spirit

I believe this is what Paul meant when he wrote, "We have the mind of Christ" (1 Corinthians 2:16) and instructed us to "put on Christ" (Galatians 3:27). He also said that we should let our minds be washed by the "water of the Word"

The inner life of a Christian is often a strange admixture of motivations, some genuinely spiritual and others completely human.

(Ephesians 5:26). We bring our soul, or conscience, to a razor sharp edge of sensitivity to the voice of God through prayer, fasting, and meditation on the written Word.

The human spirit can discern accurately the difference between right and wrong or good and evil as a result of eating from the tree of the knowledge of good and evil, from which God had forbidden man to eat. "Then the Lord God said, 'Behold, the man has become like one of Us, to know good and evil. And now, lest he put out his hand and take also of the tree of life, and eat, and live forever'" (Genesis 3:22).

For man to be able to obey and do good when evil is present, his human spirit must be subjected to both the Spirit and the Word (or law) of God. As Paul wrote in Romans 7:21-22, "I find then a law, that, when I would do good, evil is present with me. For I delight in the law of God after the inward man."[4]

In our quest to accurately discern the human spirit, we must first understand the nature of mankind. Some have used the term " tri-partite" to describe the nature of man, suggesting that man is composed of body, soul, and spirit. While this is true in theory, mankind is actually comprised of body (the flesh) and the soul/spirit, which exist in union with each other. The soul of man exists only by the spirit of life which God breathed into man. The body represents our flesh, including our senses of smelling, hearing, feeling, seeing, and tasting. It exists along with the soul/spirit. When the soul/spirit departs from the body, physical death has occurred. It is the soul/spirit that will live for eternity; they cannot be separated.

Contained within our soul/spirit are our will, our emotions, our mind, our conscience, our heart, and our life. Again, we must remember that God created the human soul/spirit with the breath of life: "And the Lord God formed man of the dust of the ground, and breathed into his nostrils the breath of life; and man became a living being" (Genesis 2:7). "Thus says the Lord, who stretches out the heavens, lays the foundation of the earth, and *forms the spirit of man within him*" (Zechariah 12:1). Without the spirit of life from God (which is our human spirit), there is no soul.

In Genesis 4 when Cain slew Abel, the Lord said, "What have you done? The voice of your brother's blood cries out to Me from the ground." (v. 4:10). Here the soul is described as the voice of Abel's blood crying out as life was leaving the flesh. When the spirit of life departs from man, the soul departs with it. They are inseparable. The soul/spirit is what returns to God.

Everyone goes to the same place. All are of the dust, and all turn to dust again. "Who knoweth the spirit of man that goeth upward, and the spirit of the beast that goeth downward to the earth? (Ecclesiastes 3:20-21)[5]

The Human Spirit

While ministering in Ohio during the summer of 1990, a young man started attending the church where I was preaching. His parents were of the Catholic faith and didn't understand anything about the Pentecostal experience. They allowed their teenage son to attend the revival services but they never came at all. One Saturday evening around midnight, the pastor received an urgent phone call from the parents of this boy. Apparently he had been playing football Saturday afternoon and while running full speed to catch a pass had run headfirst into a steel light post. The blow to his head had caused severe brain damage, and he was in a coma, perhaps near death.

The pastor called me and asked if I would go with him to pray for the boy. I paused for a moment to hear what the Spirit would say and the Lord spoke two words to me, "Go pray." By the time we arrived at the hospital, the boy had been clinically dead for four hours. We entered the waiting room where the parents were already mourning their son. I recall the mother greeting me and saying, " Hello, Father.

> *What I failed to realize was that the parents were expecting me to pray a prayer of blessing over their son, not a prayer to raise him from the dead!*

Thank you for coming to pray for our son." What I failed to realize was that the parents were expecting me to pray a prayer of blessing over their son, not a prayer to raise him from the dead!

I made my way into the room where he was lying. Tubes

and wires were strung from his body to several machines on the table. The heart and brain function monitors were silent., a flat line showing on both. A doctor was standing over the body filling out the death certificate. As I entered the room, the doctor stared at me with an annoyed look on his face. He then asked, "What do you want?" I paused. I then said, stuttering, "S-sir, I'm an evangelist and the parents of this boy asked me to pray for him." The doctor glared at me and snapped, "What for, can't you see that he's dead." I stood my ground and answered, "I still wish to pray for him, sir." The doctor then slammed his clipboard down on the table, spun on his heel, and cursed as he left the room.

There were two nurses still in the room looking at me curiously. I slowly went over to where the boy was lying and knelt down beside him. Within just a few moments I was completely immersed in intercessory prayer. I could hear the two nurses in the background whispering to each other. Undaunted, I pressed on in prayer. As I knelt there with my eyes closed, I could feel the dense heaviness of the spirit of death in that room. I could sense nothing coming from the body. No spirit. No life. No interaction. Yet I pressed on in prayer, rebuking the spirit of death and releasing the life-giving Spirit of Jesus into the room.

Thirty minutes had passed when, suddenly, in the midst of deep travail, I began to feel the spirit of death slowly beginning to lift. At the same moment I heard a commotion outside the door and realized that the cursing doctor was returning. He asked the nurses, "What's that man doing in there...someone call for security." I knew I had only a very small window of opportunity to speak the word of faith for the spirit of life to return into the body. I stood and, placing my hand on the young man's chest, spoke out, "In the name

The Human Spirit

of Jesus I command the spirit of life to return to this body!" At that very instant I felt the young man's spirit return into his body.

Immediately the monitors began to register heartbeats and brain waves, and the young man began to twist and writhe on the bed. One of the nurses screamed and, dropping her clipboard, ran out of the room. The next moment a security guard entered the room and grabbed my arm, saying, "I'm sorry, Reverend, but you'll have to leave this room immediately." As I left I could hear the doctor attempting to explain (away) to the parents how their son could have come back to life. We understand that the body was restored to life after the soul/spirit had returned as a result of my prayer of faith.

In the day of judgment man will stand before God as soul/spirit. What we do in our earthly body will be judged in our heavenly body of soul/spirit. Though this soul/spirit body will be immortal, it will still contain memories of the past life lived in the temple of flesh. We can see this in Jesus' account of the rich man and Lazarus:

> *"There was a certain rich man who was clothed in purple and fine linen and fared sumptuously every day. But there was a certain beggar named Lazarus, full of sores, who was laid at his gate, desiring to be fed with the crumbs which fell from the rich man's table. Moreover the dogs came and licked his sores. So it was that the beggar died, and was carried by the angels to Abraham's bosom. The rich man also died and was buried. And being in torments in Hades, he lifted up his eyes and saw Abraham afar off, and Lazarus in his bosom. Then he cried and said, 'Father Abraham, have mercy on me, and send Lazarus*

that he may dip the tip of his finger in water and cool my tongue; for I am tormented in this flame.' But Abraham said, 'Son, remember that in your lifetime you received your good things, and likewise Lazarus evil things; but now he is comforted and you are tormented. And besides all this, between us and you there is a great gulf fixed, so that those who want to pass from here to you cannot, nor can those from there pass to us.' Then he said, 'I beg you therefore, father, that you would send him to my father's house, for I have five brothers, that he may testify to them, lest they also come to this place of torment'" (Luke 16:19-28).

The true character and state of a man will shine forth from his human spirit.

It is evident from this passage that the rich man had complete memory of his life on earth in the afterlife.

In his first letter to the church in Thessalonica, Paul wrote, "Now may the God of peace Himself sanctify you completely; and may your whole spirit, soul, and body be preserved blameless at the coming of our Lord Jesus Christ" (1 Thessalonians 5:23). He also wrote concerning the first man (the man of both flesh and soul/spirit) and the second man (soul/spirit):

*So also is the resurrection of the dead. It is sown in **corruption**; it is raised in **incorruption**: It is sown in* *dishonor; it is raised in glory: it is sown in weakness; it is raised in power: It is sown a **natural body**; it is raised a **spiritual body**. There is a natural body, and there is a spiritual body. And so it is written, The first man Adam was made a living soul; the last Adam was made a quickening spirit. Howbeit that was not first which is spiritual, but that which is natural; and afterward that which is spiritual. The first man is of the earth, earthy: the second man is the Lord from heaven. As is the earthy, such are they also that are earthy: and as is the heavenly, such are they also that are heavenly. And as we have borne the image of the earthy, we shall also bear the image of the heavenly. Now this I say, brethren, that flesh and blood cannot inherit the kingdom of God; neither doth corruption inherit incorruption* (1 Corinthians 15:42-50) [6]

A man can model any behavior, character, personality, or appearance through the flesh and soul (as actors are so well trained to do), but the human spirit ultimately shines forth in a man, communicating the true character of his soul. "For as he thinketh in his heart, so is he" (Proverbs 23:7).[7] "The spirit of a man is the lamp of the Lord, searching all the inner depths of his heart" (Proverbs 20:27).

When the true character of a man is shining forth, this is where discerning the spirit of a man becomes a necessary part of ministry. I have had people shake my hand with a great big smile on their face, modeling good intentions and sincere motives, whereas through the gift of discerning of spirits I have discerned hatred, jealousy, or a desire to do harm emanating from their human spirit. Dealing with people according to what their human spirit is projecting has saved me many heartaches and much trouble. On occasion, ignoring what is all too evident in their human spirit has caused me much pain and difficulty.

Wisdom and understanding are also perceived through the human spirit. Knowledge is gained through the soul functions. This is why there are young men and women who have obtained wisdom beyond their years through fasting and prayer, procuring this wisdom directly from God. When a young man dedicates his youthful years to fasting and much time spent alone with God in prayer and meditation on the Word of God, he gains the wisdom of the Spirit. Even a young man can become "old" through hours of fasting and prayer and gain great wisdom from God. This wisdom does not come from earthly knowledge, gray hair, or the lack thereof—it comes from God. James wrote concerning this wisdom from above, "If any of you lacks wisdom, let him ask of God, who gives to all liberally and without reproach, and it will be given to him" (James 1:5). This is the same kind of wisdom King Solomon received from God in his youth:

> *Now the king went to Gibeon to sacrifice there, for that was the great high place: Solomon offered a thousand*

The world will be greatly affected in this last hour by those who have gained the wisdom from God through these measures of commitment.

> *burnt offerings on that altar. At Gibeon the Lord appeared to Solomon in a dream by night; and God said,*

*"Ask! What shall I give you?" And Solomon said: "You have shown great mercy to Your servant David my father, because he walked before You in truth, in righteousness, and in uprightness of heart with You; You have continued this great kindness for him, and You have given him a son to sit on his throne, as it is this day. "Now, O Lord my God, You have made Your servant king instead of my father David, but I am a little child; I do not know how to go out or come in. "And Your servant is in the midst of Your people whom You have chosen, a great people, too numerous to be numbered or counted. "Therefore give to Your servant an **understanding heart** to judge Your people, that I may discern between good and evil. For who is able to judge this great people of Yours?" The speech pleased the Lord, that Solomon had asked this thing. Then God said to him: "Because you have asked this thing, and have not asked long life for yourself, nor have asked riches for yourself, nor have asked the life of your enemies, but have asked for yourself understanding to discern justice, behold, I have done according to your words; see, **I have given you a wise and understanding heart, so that there has not been anyone like you before you, nor shall any like you arise after you*** (1 Kings 3:4-12).

This same principle applies to those who are old in natural years but have never submitted their human spirit to prayer, fasting, and obedience to the Word and Spirit of God. These people tend to be foolish and immature in the ways and wisdom of the Spirit.

Think of it, the wisdom of the Spirit of God has no

boundaries or limitations. The omniscient God will share His "secrets" with all who come to know Him intimately. "Surely the Lord GOD will do nothing, but he revealeth his secret unto his servants the prophets" (Amos 3:7).[8]

If we will purpose in our hearts to seek the Lord through much time alone with Him and much fasting, He will reveal His wisdom in our lives. The world will be greatly affected in this last hour by those who have gained the wisdom from God through these measures of commitment. Pray right now for the Lord to begin to endow you with the wisdom of His Spirit.

Endnotes for Chapter 4:

---

i. *The King James Version*, (Cambridge: Cambridge, 1769).

ii. *Enhanced Strong's Lexicon*, (Oak Harbor, WA: Logos Research Systems, Inc., 1995).

iii. Ibid.

4. *The King James Version*, (Cambridge: Cambridge, 1769).

5. Ibid.

6. Ibid.

7. Ibid.

8. Ibid.

EPILOGUE

The Spirits of this Age

"When an unclean spirit goes out of a man, he goes through dry places, seeking rest, and finds none. Then he says, 'I will return to my house from which I came.' And when he comes, he finds it empty, swept, and put in order. Then he goes and takes with him seven other spirits more wicked than himself, and they enter and dwell there; and the last state of that man is worse than the first. **So shall it also be with this wicked generation***"* (Matthew 12:43-45).

I have been asked many times by those who have an aversion to being filled with the Holy Ghost evidenced by speaking in tongues, "Do I really need to be filled with the Holy Spirit?" We must first understand that the spirits of this

Epilogue: The Spirits of this Age

age will be seven times greater than in the first generation. Do we need to be filled with Holy Ghost? I believe that not only is it essential for salvation, but without the overcoming power of Holy Ghost within we will not make it in this last hour against the spirits that will be unleashed upon this world. The greatest protection we can have in this last hour is the protection of knowing our names are recorded in the book of life—an active, working salvation.

> *Then the seventy returned with joy, saying, "Lord, even the demons are subject to us in Your name." And He said to them, "I saw Satan fall like lightning from heaven. Behold, I give you the authority to trample on serpents and scorpions, and over all the power of the enemy, and nothing shall by any means hurt you. Nevertheless do not rejoice in this, that the spirits are subject to you, but rather rejoice because your names are written in heaven"* (Luke 10:17-20).

It is easy to do the work of God when it is making us look good or serving to benefit us materially.

The spirits of this age are so diverse that I will not make an attempt to cover them all. I will cover a few, however, that I believe are spirits indicative of this age we live in. We can find some of the spirits of this age described in the Revelation letters to the seven churches.

And to the angel of the church in Pergamos write, 'These

things says He who has the sharp two-edged sword: "I know your works, and where you dwell, where Satan's throne is. And you hold fast to My name, and did not deny My faith even in the days in which Antipas was My faithful martyr, who was killed among you, where Satan dwells. But I have a few things against you, because you have there those who hold the doctrine of Balaam, who taught Balak to put a stumbling block before the children of Israel, to eat things sacrificed to idols, and to commit sexual immorality. Thus you also have those who hold the doctrine of the Nicolaitans, which thing I hate (Revelation 2:12-15).

Verse 14 describes the first spirit of this age I would like to cover: the spirit of Balaam. This spirit is characterized by greed, deception, and false doctrine, all in the name of religion. This spirit will cause a minister to replace a sincere burden for souls and with a sincere desire for a larger pay check. It will even deceive a minister into believing it is perfectly all right to practice immorality, to steal, to lie, to cheat, to gossip, or to slander his brother, so long as it serves his personal agenda. I have seen the spirit of Balaam cause a pastor to counsel a young convert to sell a portion of the cocaine he had from a former lifestyle so the church could be "blessed" financially. The spirit of Balaam always reasons that the end justifies the means (*I write more on this in The Mantle of God*).

We must become servants to the burden of the Lord!

This spirit often disguises itself behind a host of good works. It is easy to do the work of God when it is making us look good or serving to benefit us materially. This spirit can deceive an entire church into hoarding up its financial resources for its own security and strength while the work of God both nationally and internationally goes suffers great want. What those who are deceived by the spirit of Balaam do not understand is that God gives true authority and blesses when we pour ourselves out with a true burden into the work of the Lord.

Jacob's prophecy to his sons foretold that the descendants of Issachar would rise above their personal desires and become servants of the burden:

> *"Issachar is a strong donkey, lying down between two burdens; he saw that rest was good, and that the land was pleasant;* **he bowed his shoulder to bear a burden**, *and became a band of slaves"* (Genesis 49:14-15).

We must be willing to truly serve the burden of the work of God, not ourselves, our ministries, or our churches—only the burden. Years after the tribe of Issachar became a band of burden-bearers, God lifted them up in authority and anointing over the other eleven tribes.

> *Of the sons of Issachar who had understanding of the times, to know what Israel ought to do, their chiefs were two hundred; and all their brethren were at their command* (1 Chronicles 12:32).

We must become servants to the burden of the Lord!

Revelation 2:15 speaks of the spirit of the Nicolaitans. The Nicolaitans were advocates of "free love" and "false grace" during the era of the first church. They were the first to redefine grace as a licence to sin and commit immorality with guaranteed, continual forgiveness from God. They deceived the church into participation in many of the Greco-Roman love feasts. Open immorality and homosexuality often occurred at these feasts. They also were some of the first to compromise the New Testament churches doctrine with an acceptance of pagan beliefs and false doctrine. This is supported by *The Bible Knowledge Commentary* and *Harper's Bible Dictionary*.

Nicolaitans (ni-koh-lay×i-tahns), a religious sect in Ephesus and Pergamum whose members were denounced in Rev. 2:6, 15 for eating food sacrificed to idols and for sexual license. The church fathers considered them followers of Nicolaus of Antioch mentioned in Acts 6:5 and founders of libertine Gnosticism, which remained active beyond the second century. See also Revelation to John, The; Ephesus; Pergamum.[i]

Epilogue: The Spirits of this Age

They were also condemned for following the Nicolaitans' teaching. Earlier the Ephesian church had been commended for rejecting what appears to be a moral departure (cf. Rev. 2:6). Some Greek manuscripts add here that God hates the teaching of the Nicolaitans, as also stated in v. 6. Compromise with worldly morality and pagan doctrine was

---
These abominable practices are not sicknesses at all. They are sin!

---

prevalent in the church, especially in the third century when Christianity became popular. So compromise with pagan morality and departure from biblical faith soon corrupted the church.[ii]

In this last hour, the spirit of the Nicolaitans is trying to assert its deceptive views into church teachings, advocating tolerance and acceptance of homosexuality, lesbianism, drug use, alcohol use, and many other sins as a incurable genetic sicknesses. These abominable practices are not sicknesses at all. They are sin!

The spirit of the Nicolaitans also is trying to introduce the notion of a one-world Body of Christ composed of all beliefs. Every year in the month of September, the World Parliament of Religions provides a platform for the spirit of the Nicolaitans to speak its deceptions. At this meeting so-called Christians, Buddhists, Hindus, Moslems, New Agers, and even members of the occult gather to end the narrow differences of the conservative church and bring religious unity for the cause of world community. Revelations 13:11-

12 speaks of this kind of religious unity:

> *Then I saw another beast coming up out of the earth, and he had two horns like a lamb and spoke like a dragon. And he exercises all the authority of the first beast in his presence,* **and causes the earth and those who dwell in it to worship the first beast**, *whose deadly wound was healed.*

All who become deceived by the spirit of the Nicolaitans and do not repent will be swept into the whirlpool of deception and will find themselves right in the lap of the Harlot, worshiping the beast with all deceived faiths.

A common statement I hear from those who have been swept into deception, and joined themselves with those in false doctrine is, "How can God not be with them with all the healing, miracles, signs, and wonders in their midst?" We must remember that some of the spirits of this age have great power to perform signs, wonders, and miracles:

> *And I saw three unclean spirits like frogs coming out of the mouth of the dragon, out of the mouth of the beast, and out of the mouth of the false prophet. For they are spirits of demons, performing signs, which go out to the kings of the earth and of the whole world, to gather them to the battle of that great day of God Almighty* (Revelation 16:13-14).

The old adage, "You do not follow signs, wonders, and miracles; they follow you as you follow Jesus" will become invaluable counsel for the church beset by the spirit of the Nicolaitans.

Epilogue: The Spirits of this Age

Revelation 2:20 speaks of the spirit of Jezebel and the curses that have resulted from this spirit:

"Nevertheless I have a few things against you, because you allow that woman Jezebel, who calls herself a

---

The old adage, "You do not follow signs, wonders, and miracles; they follow you as you follow Jesus" will become invaluable counsel for the church beset by the spirit of the Nicolaitans.

---

prophetess, to teach and seduce My servants to commit sexual immorality and eat things sacrificed to idols. And I gave her time to repent of her sexual immorality, and she did not repent. Indeed I will cast her into a sickbed, and those who commit adultery with her into great tribulation, unless they repent of their deeds. I will kill her children with death, and all the churches shall know that I am He who searches the minds and hearts. And I will give to each one of you according to your works.

The sickbed and great tribulation spoken of in verse 22 is AIDS and all the sexually transmitted diseases of this hour. The Women's Liberation Movement is mostly responsible for the Pro-Choice Movement and the ensuing slaughter of millions of unborn children. The spirit of Jezebel is the invisible force that drives these movements (*I write in more detail about this in the book "The Spirit of Jezebel".*)

God never intended men and women to be identical. They were created different in body, mind, emotion, and many other areas. The spirit of Jezebel attempts blur the divine line that God has established in order to destroy the umbrella of authority in the home. This brings chaos to home life and ultimately produce dysfunctional households. This is all to strengthen the spirits of perversion in this hour. I believe the domineering, unsubmitted, overpowering spirit of Jezebel is responsible, at least in part, for the sprit of homosexuality which plagues the moral fiber of the world. Nothing is more beautiful and comforting than to observe a home set in biblical order according to Paul's writings in Colossians 3:18-20: "Wives, submit to your own husbands, as is fitting in the Lord. Husbands, love your wives and do not be bitter toward them. Children, obey your parents in all things, for this is well pleasing to the Lord.

Revelation 3:14-18 contains the most subtle and deceptive spirit of this age, the spirit of Laodicea;

> *"And to the angel of the church of the Laodiceans write, 'These things says the Amen, the Faithful and True Witness, the Beginning of the creation of God: "I know your works, that you are neither cold nor hot. I could wish you were cold or hot. So then, because you are lukewarm, and neither cold nor hot, I will vomit you out of My mouth. Because you say, 'I am rich, have become wealthy, and have need of nothing'—and do not know that you are wretched, miserable, poor, blind, and naked— I counsel you to buy from Me gold refined in the*

fire, that you may be rich; and white garments, that you may be clothed, that the shame of your nakedness may not be revealed; and anoint your eyes with eye salve, that you may see.

This spirit attempts to blind the New Testament church to

> **It deceives believers, causing them to fall into the snare of materialism, entertainment, and selfish greed while the world dies and goes to hell in a handbasket.**

the desperate need of the hour to spread the gospel. It seeks to rob the church of relationship and intimacy with God. It deceives believers, causing them to fall into the snare of materialism, entertainment, and selfish greed while the world dies and goes to hell in a handbasket. So many are deceived by this subtle spirit, because it does not seem to be as wicked as the other spirits of this age. But, this spirit is the most dangerous as it saps the spiritual strength from the church and is almost immune to the conviction of the Word and Spirit of God.

I pray this book stirs us to repentance again and to buy the gold refined in the fire of prayer, fasting, and serving the burden of the Lord. I pray that it stirs us to obtain the riches of the Spirit and eternal verities. Let us vigorously resist the spirits of this age drawing nigh unto God, that we may be clothed with the pure white garments of His righteousness and holiness.

Oh Lord, anoint our eyes, our ears, and our hearts, that we may discern the way that is pleasing to you.

Let us vigorously resist the spirits of this age drawing nigh unto God, that we may be clothed with the pure white garments of His righteousness and holiness.

Endnotes for Epilogue:

i. Achtemier, Paul J., Th.D., *Harper's Bible Dictionary* (San Francisco: Harper and Row, Publishers, Inc.,1985), pp.112

ii. Walvoord, John F., and Zuck, Roy B., *The Bible Knowledge Commentary* (Wheaton, Illinois: Scripture Press Publications, Inc., 1983, 1985), pp.941

OTHER MATERIALS BY JOHN ARCOVIO

The Way of the Eagle
Spiritual principles and the operation of spiritual gifts are illustrated through this fascinating portrait of an eagle in the wild. You will mount up with the wings of an eagle as you read. (Available in Spanish and French)

$15.00 each includes shipping

Three Warfares
Before genuine apostolic revival will ever sweep across our nation, the American Church will have to come to grips with three dimensions of spiritual warfare. Arm yourself and charge headlong into the battle as you read this book

$15.00 each includes shipping

The Mantle of God
The prophets of old were identified and protected by the unique mantle they wore. Discover the New Testament believer's mantle, made also for identification and protection. Take it upon you as you read and wear it to the glory of God!

$15.00 each includes shipping

Discerning the Spirits of this End-Time Apostolic Age
As the coming of the Lord approaches and we prepare to cross the threshold into the 21st century, it is my conviction that the church must possess the operation of the gift of discerning of spirits that Paul wrote about in 2 Corinthians 12:10. This book will enlighten you in the area of discernment of the spirits of this hour.

$15.00 each includes shipping

The Other Side of Pentecost
The Other Side of Pentecost is a compilation of humorous stories that John Arcovio has heard, observed, or experienced while ministering in churches around the world. May this lighthearted look at Pentecost serve you much medicine.

$10.00 each includes shipping

Thoughts From Above
An eight-tape series dealing with prayer, fasting, the operation of spiritual gifts, and principles concerning the fivefold ministry.

$45.00 each includes shipping

Thoughts From Above Part II
An six-tape series dealing with principles concerning apostolic authority , an in-depth questions and answers session concerning the fivefold ministry and the spirit realm.

$35.00 each includes shipping

Personal Evangelism 101 Soulwinning Seminar
A "one-on-one ministry" Soulwinning seminar that will challenge your faith and stir your heart to a greater burden for the lost. Comes with a 90-minute cassette tape and a 16-page, easy-to-follow booklet. (Available in Spanish)

$20.00 each includes shipping

Prayer and Fasting Seminar
Prayer and Fasting are two sure means by which the believer can gain access to God through a direct line to heaven. You will be blessed by this anointed teaching. Two cassette tapes.

$20.00 each includes shipping

Destroying Spiritual Yokes
Isaiah 10:17 records, "And it shall come to pass in that day, that his burden shall be taken away from off thy shoulder, and his yoke from off thy neck, and the yoke shall be destroyed because of the anointing." Many Christians, though forgiven from a sinful past, still struggle with many spiritual yokes as a result of the forgiven sins. This teaching series will enlighten you on the reality of spiritual deliverance from these yokes thru the power of the Spirit. Two cassette tapes.

$20.00 each includes shipping

Activating the Gifts of the Spirit
The nine gifts of the spirit found listed in 1 Corinthians Chapter 12 are not exclusively for the ministry but also for operation among the Body of Christ. This is valuable teaching on what activates the nine gifts in a persons life. Two cassette tapes and syllabus.

$20.00 each includes shipping

The Forgiveness Factor

Unforgiveness is a prison many are locked in. Experience the power these revelatory tapes will release into your life to truly "walk in the Spirit of freedom." Also, hear John Arcovio=s heart captivating and transforming personal testimony. Six cassette tapes.

$40.00 each includes shipping

How To Conduct Holy Ghost Crusades

A "step-by-step" instructional video on the inner working of crusades. This video contains live shots of actual crusades conducted by John Arcovio. Also witness blind eyes opened, deaf ears unstopped, the lame walking, the demon-possessed delivered, and thousands being instantaneously filled with the Holy Spirit.

$20.00 each includes shipping

Endtime Prophecy Video Seminar (4 Videos)

Four 60 min powerful videos taught by Pastor John Arcovio on the 1. Seven Trumpets, 2. The mark of The Beast,3. The Harlot Church and 4.The Four Horsemen. You will be amazed at the prophetic revelations taught in these series.

$20.00 each includes shipping

The Spirit of Jezebel

Three Part Series on exposing, and defeating The spirit of jezebel. Three 60 minute CD's

$20.00 each includes shipping

Visit our website at http://www.spiritled.org for updated information on ministry materials.